SERIES XLIII   No. 2

JOHNS HOPKINS UNIVERSITY STUDIES

IN

HISTORICAL AND POLITICAL SCIENCE

Under the Direction of the

Departments of History, Political Economy, and
Political Science

THE VIRGINIA FRONTIER, 1754-1763

BY

LOUIS K. KOONTZ, PH. D.

Instructor in History, University of California

BALTIMORE
THE JOHNS HOPKINS PRESS
1925

Maryland
With Pride

Facsimile Reprint

Published 1992 By

HERITAGE BOOKS, INC.
1540E Pointer Ridge Place, Bowie, Maryland 20716
(301) 390-7709

ISBN 1-55613-663-3

PREFACE

The existing material for a study of the Virginia Frontier
during the French and Indian War is relatively accessible.
The printed sources are of course familiar to the average
student. These include the provincial records of the several
colonies, particularly Massachusetts, New York, Pennsylvania, Maryland, Virginia, and the Carolinas. They are
to be found in every important library in the country. In
Virginia we have the Journals of the House of Burgesses,
the Council records, the colonial laws, the Augusta County
records, vestry records, newspaper files, the papers and writings of Washington, letters to Washington, and miscellaneous
data in numerous county histories, the Calendar of Virginia
State Papers, the Dinwiddie Papers, the Virginia Magazine
of History and Biography, and minor historical publications. Unfortunately, there are many gaps in the records
that cannot be bridged because important materials have been
lost or destroyed. For example, Virginia sustained irre-
parable loss when fire in 1781 destroyed practically all manuscript material bearing on the French and Indian War
which was then in the State Library. The State archives
of Virginia contain no journals or even rough minutes
of the council sessions between May 6, 1743, and March 4,
1768.

The manuscript material on the French and Indian War
period to be found in Virginia is scattered about in private
hands. Occasionally the historian is fortunate enough to
discover some of it. Undoubtedly there are some papers
held by individuals in adjoining States, but this material is
probably negligible.

There are, however, three modern depositories outside
the State that hold matter on this period that is vital. The
first of these is the Library of Congress. It possesses considerable manuscript matter bearing on the French and
Indian War, notably in the collection of the Washington

v

Papers. The second depository is that of the splendid Henry E. Huntington Library at San Marino, near Los Angeles, California, which has acquired the indispensable Brock Collection, as well as the Loudoun, Abercrombie, and other important papers. The writer found that in the main this material serves chiefly to corroborate the statements and facts already accessible to him in the published papers and writings of Washington and in the Draper collection of manuscripts. The third important source of unpublished material on the Virginia Frontier during the French and Indian War is the collection of Draper Manuscripts in the library of the State Historical Society of Wisconsin. The greater part of this material was once scattered over Virginia and adjoining States, but was gathered together during travels lasting through many years, by that indefatigable historical collector, Dr. Lyman C. Draper. For the purposes of this study the writer has had the privilege of making a systematic examination of this entire collection. The Preston and Virginia Papers yielded the most important material in this collection.

It will be observed that at certain points in this study extended quotations or entire letters have been included in the body of the text. The reason for this is that the extracts are, as a rule, taken from previously unused source material.

Acknowledgment of indebtedness for aid in the preparation of these pages is due to the following persons: It was at the suggestion of Professor John H. Latané, of the Johns Hopkins University, that this investigation was undertaken, and it was carried forward with the help of his encouragement and cooperation. Most discriminating suggestions were offered by Dr. Louise P. Kellogg, of the State Historical Society of Wisconsin. Miss Mabel C. Weeks, one-time chief of the division of maps and manuscripts in the same society, has frequently been called upon for assistance in reading, evaluation, and in photostating the Draper Manuscripts. Professor Charles M. Andrews, of Yale University, encouraged the writer by emphasizing the timeliness of such a study as this and in indicating attitude and method of treatment. To Hon. Houston G. Young, formerly Secretary of State of West Virginia, the author is indebted for indispensable reports from the West Virginia archives. The library staff of the Johns Hopkins University, that of the Peabody Institute, Baltimore, and that of the Henry E. Huntington Library have generously extended every possible courtesy to the author in the preparation of this study. Mrs. S. R. Gammon, Jr., formerly library assistant in the departments of History and Political Science in the Johns Hopkins University, has aided the author in securing important bibliographical data. To Miss Marjorie Russell, formerly with the war-time Federal Trade Commission, and Miss Elizabeth Hoke, at the same time with the Air Service, U. S. Army, indebtedness is gratefully acknowledged for the endless tedium of typing and retyping the manuscript and accompanying documents. Thanks are due to Mr. J. C. Fitzpatrick, acting chief of the division of manuscripts, Library of Congress, for information and suggestions in connection with the use of the Washington Manuscripts in that library. John O. Knott, Ph. D., chautauqua lecturer, has read the manuscript of this study and has offered valuable suggestions as to arrangement and style.

L. K. K.

TABLE OF CONTENTS

THE VIRGINIA FRONTIER, 1754-1763

CHAPTER I

INTRODUCTION

It is surprising that there has not been prepared hitherto a study of the Virginia Frontier covering the critical years of the French and Indian War. There have been indeed numerous monographs upon phases of this subject but no comprehensive treatment of the field as a whole. Every general book on American history with any pretense to thoroughness devotes a few pages to frontier conditions during this period. There are many volumes that touch phases of the subject as is evident upon examination of the bibliography. The object, therefore, of this investigation is to present a coordinated picture of the American pioneer between, approximately, 1754 and 1763, with the emphasis upon the Virginia Frontier. To do this it has been necessary to study the physiographical conditions of the frontier country, to trace the steps in the westward advance of the colonists, to analyze the reasons for that advance, and to give some account of the racial and religious groups in this connection.

In order to give the Virginia Frontier its proper historical setting in the time of which we write, it has been necessary to make brief mention of concurrent events in European history, and to devote considerable space to conditions in all of the American colonies at this period, particularly to those colonies adjacent to Virginia. Neither chance nor fancy is responsible for the selection of the Virginia Frontier as a subject for research in contradistinction to the frontier of any other American colony. Virginia was a centrally located province, and thus enjoyed the advantage of position. It was furthermore the oldest of the colonies, had the largest area, and was the most populous of the British North American possessions—deriving from all these advantages a certain prestige above the neighboring colonies. Furthermore, it was the fate of the Virginia colony, on account of the extent and situation of its frontier, to be brought in contact with the ambitious French to the west and north, particularly after the organization of the Ohio Company. This contact with the French carried with it contact with Indians whom the French had won to their way of thinking. Virginia sent the first message to the French when that nation encroached upon British territory, and Virginia fired the first shot in the French and Indian War.

It was Virginia's fortune, or misfortune, to have within her bounds the disputed " Gateway to the West" at the " Forks of the Ohio," the control of which was essential to the interests of both the English and the French. Thus Virginia was sure to be the first of the colonies to feel the force of French intrigue and French hostility to British rule west of the Alleghanies. Not only so, but the extent of Virginia's territory, though expressed in somewhat vague terms, meant the retention or loss for England of what we now regard as a section of the United States second to no other in wealth and desirability. When we recall that Virginia's frontier extended from the " Forks of the Ohio " (now Pittsburgh, Pennsylvania) to the borders of the Carolinas, and that the entire grant included territory from the Atlantic Ocean to the Mississippi River,[1] we appreciate what was involved in the contention with the French for land granted to the Ohio Company as part of the vast area which Virginia laid claim to in the Ohio and Mississippi valleys. Of course, the term " Mississippi River " meant at the time nothing very definite to men of England or even to the colonists of Virginia. But this makes all the more interesting the struggle in which Virginia took the lead; as a matter of fact, the colonists were contending for far more than they understood at the time.

During this period Virginia contributed one man of great resourcefulness to whom America owes a lasting debt—Robert Dinwiddie. These pages will indicate to any candid student

---

[1] See below, p. 60.

of history that despite Governor Dinwiddie's faults, and particularly his want of tact in connection with the famous "pistole fee dispute" and his attitude toward Washington in regard to Fort Cumberland, he was probably the strongest colonial governor in the colonies at the period of the French and Indian War, and certainly the most persistent and resourceful in devising ways and means to save the North American continent for the English people.

Closely associated with Governor Dinwiddie, but ultimately eclipsing him in both statesmanship and service to the colonies and to the country in the after days, stands the great Virginian whom it was Dinwiddie's fortune to discover. Probably the words of an English historian express as forcibly and as justly as any writer the significance of Dinwiddie's selection of George Washington, then a youth of twenty-one, to bear the initial message to the French commander on the extreme frontier of disputed territory, telling the French to withdraw. Doyle says of this selection of Washington for the proposed errand: "No one short of an inspired prophet could have foreseen that Dinwiddie's selection of Washington was putting the young land surveyor on the first step of a career full of greatness. All that we can say is that out of all the young and enterprising Virginians available for such a mission, Dinwiddie chose the one fittest." [2]

It will be noted that the later years of the period under discussion are covered much less fully than the earlier ones. The author has attempted to present typical events, questions and issues—those that involve what was basic and vital to an understanding of the times and the significance of the occurrences narrated. It will be seen that the topical method has been followed as far as possible. If there are disadvantages in this method of treatment, the author has considered that the advantages outweigh the disadvantages. Topical treatment lends itself more readily to the story form of writing which has been followed as far as practicable in this

---

[2] J. A. Doyle, English Colonies in America, vol. v, p. 430.

entire treatment until the chapter on the frontier Forts is introduced.

The preliminary chapter on Topography is intended as background merely. Such books as Semple's "American History and Its Geographic Conditions" have covered the field of physical environment and topography so well that nothing more has been thought necessary in this work than to state the principles already enunciated in such books, in their application to movements which bear upon the matter in this volume.

There may be sincere objection to placing undue emphasis upon the years of the French and Indian War before war was really declared, and dismissing with a comparatively few pages the account of that struggle when Pitt had come into power and death blows were being dealt to the French cause. But as this study is confined to the Virginia Frontier, stress is laid upon events relating more exclusively to that frontier. Not only so, but the years to which space is given in this study are the years during which Virginia carried the burden of the war, even though the formal declaration of war had not yet been made. It was a Virginia Governor, Dinwiddie, who, from the time he entered upon his office to the close of his term, had one thought only, to which he gave his time and powers—that of deciding for all time the rights of the British to the American territory east of the Mississippi River. He forced the question to the front, began the war, conducted it almost single-handed until Braddock was sent to the rescue, retrieved as far as possible the disaster of Braddock, and laid down his work for another to take up, only after he had developed the greatest commander of forces that the epoch produced, and one of the greatest of all time. Furthermore, Dinwiddie had so fortified the Virginia Frontier as to render the protecting of it a comparatively simple matter. Virginia had "done her part" even had she done no more than she did in the years 1752–1756. In April, 1757, Dinwiddie, who could not be charged with undue partiality for Virginia, wrote to Pitt these words:

" In justice to this dominion I must inform you they've been more attentive to his majesty's commands and supporting his just rights than any other Colony on this continent." [3]

The chapter on the Forts of the Frontier contains much that has hitherto remained unpublished. The matter is somewhat detached from the main story of colonial defense which gathers largely about the personalities of Governor Dinwiddie and Colonel George Washington, but it is eminently desirable that the fortified positions should be positively identified and the chronicle of their development authoritatively established.

---

[3] Dinwiddie Papers, vol. ii, p. 642, quoted by H. R. McIlwaine, Journals of the House of Burgesses, 1752-1758, p. xxviii.

CHAPTER II

Seen from an airplane and by means of specially adapted optical instruments, the Appalachian mountain system of America would appear like a series of huge earthen fortifications stretching in lines from Vermont to Alabama running in parallels and differing in heights. From our airplane we would see immense gaps in these fortifications that would have the appearance of roadways. Through many of these gaps we could discern mountain torrents like strands of silver flowing towards the Atlantic or westward towards the Mississippi River. Some of these streams gather volume as they proceed until they become wide expanses of water bearing the commerce of the nation. We would be impressed at once with the tendency of the fortification-like mountain chain to recede from the ocean as it made its way to the south. Immense plains would be discerned along the Atlantic coast extending for miles back to where the mountains began to lift up their barriers as though to forbid intrusion. An observer unacquainted with American history might infer that rival nations dwelt on opposite sides of this great fortification of nature and used the barrier for mutual protection as well as for a boundary line to define their mutual limits. But the many gaps noted in the line of defense would at once suggest that either nation could reach the other through these roadways of nature to contend for the possession of the territory of the other.

This imaginary airplane excursion may serve to put concretely before us the facts of history in relation to the early colonization of America. The English-speaking people of Europe held the Atlantic coast from the far North to the borders of Florida. The French laid claim to the vast country now known as the Mississippi Valley. The Appalachian mountains were, in truth, a natural fortification, and

the gaps in the mountains through which rivers had cut
their way, or through which in the early days the Indians
made warpaths, did in reality tempt the rival nations to reach
each other that they might contend for disputed territory on
their borders, or for stretches of territory which each claimed
by right of discovery.

For the purpose of this study it is only necessary to say
that England laid claim to much territory in the New World
that France claimed. Both nations claimed vast tracts of
country beyond the Appalachian range by flimsy titles. Taking into consideration the enmity that had existed for years
between the two nations, and the further fact that the colonists in America understood, as the people in Europe could
not, what the future of this country would mean to the
individual pioneer as well as to the nation that he represented, a decisive war between the English and the French
in America was inevitable. Our story concerns the Virginia
Frontier in this conflict, but the Virginia Frontier can not
be wholly disassociated from the entire colonial border of the
English-speaking colonists.

The gaps and depressions in the great Appalachian mountain range tempted the more adventurous of the Atlantic
Coast settlers to move westward. Once on the ground west
of the mountains, with an almost infinite stretch of virgin
country awaiting the hand of civilization, it is no wonder
that settlers would not readily yield the territory to flimsy
claims based on reputed discovery.

The first great gap in the Appalachian range as seen in
coming from the North is that made by the Hudson River.
The Hudson is three hundred miles long and is now navigable for steamers for one hundred and fifty-one miles from
its mouth; furthermore, the Mohawk River, a tributary to the
Hudson, flows from the West eastward for one hundred and
thirty-five miles, with a fall of only five hundred feet. The
Hudson to the North penetrated into the country of the
French; and to the West, by the Mohawk, it reached its
arm towards the Great Lakes region. Here we have an

example of what a channel cut by nature through a great mountain system meant to pioneers unprotected by forts, when they had to the North and to the West of them enemies, both French and Indian. No wonder that a descent upon New York's coastal territory by way of the Hudson was always in early days a danger to be considered.

But a waterway of such importance as that of the Hudson and its tributaries usually implies depressions in the mountains which feed the rivers. These depressions make travel easy and thus tempt it. As a consequence we find that waterways with accompanying mountain depressions were usually, if not invariably, the places in the forests of North America where Indian trails were to be found. Thus the famous war-trail of the Iroquois Indians led from the Hudson River up the Mohawk Valley and on to the West as far as the Great Lakes. That which was the natural way for an Indian to take in his war enterprises was the natural way for civilization to take in its advance into a forest country.[1] But the way to the West was also a way from the West. Hence the riverways and the Indian trails, in the days of which we write, while gateways of opportunity for conquest on the part of settlers on the Atlantic Coast, were also portals of entrance from the West upon any unprotected territory on the eastern slope of the country.

In close connection with roadways to the West and East through the Appalachian mountains, must be mentioned the attitude of the Indians that dwelt in the regions through which these routes led. As an example of this we find that the powerful Iroquois Indian tribes that largely controlled the Mohawk Valley route were friendly to the English nation. To keep these Indians friendly was the purpose of the English colonists; to alienate them from the English colonists was the purpose of the French. What was true in the Mohawk Valley was true, in principle, in regard to all the Indian tribes. They were courted, frightened, bought—any-

---

[1] The Mohawk Valley was to be the route of the Erie Canal and later of the New York Central railway.

thing that the emergency dictated, that might win them to neutrality if not to actual comradeship in war against a white foe.

What was true of the Hudson waterway and its tributaries to the North was true of the Susquehanna and its tributaries (particularly the Juniata) to the South. The place where Pittsburgh, Pennsylvania, now stands was then known as the Forks of the Ohio and was regarded as the Great Gateway to the West. Two routes from Philadelphia, one by the West Branch of the Susquehanna and the other by the way of the Juniata Branch, met at this gateway. These routes used by the savages of by-gone days marked the way which the white man afterwards followed,[2]—only too often to drive the Indian from his more eastern hunting ground farther and farther to the West.

In connection with the Susquehanna routes to the West we find what was true of other routes to the South. Passages to the West were generally zigzag paths, for the shortest distance between two points is not always a straight line. If mountains rear up their forms just in front of the traveler, yet open up great gaps farther south or north, and if lateral valleys invite easy passage to the gaps in the mountains, the most natural way to take in going to and from the West is the zigzag course. This, in fact, was done by the wise use of the hint which nature had given, and which the wild man of the American forest had utilized already. Probably the most famous and the most popular of all the routes to the West in the days of the French and Indian War was the one by way of the Potomac River, out through the Cumberland, Maryland, gap, and thus to the Forks of the Ohio.[3] Here again, Indian trail met and crossed Indian trail. We shall see why the English colonists fortified this route and why Virginia was so much concerned with it as a passageway to the West, and why its destination, the Great Gateway, was a nerve center throughout the entire contest be-

---

[2] Now the general route of the Pennsylvania lines.
[3] Route of the Baltimore and Ohio Railroad.

tween the French and their Indian allies and the English and their Indian adherents. The point between the branches of the Ohio was a veritable mountain Gibraltar. Washington's quick eye saw the value of this strategic point, which became the location of the afterwards famous Fort Duquesne, later Fort Pitt, and finally Pittsburgh.

Farther South than the Potomac waterway lay the James-New-Kanawha route, as it is aptly called. This route led West across the Valley of Virginia, on through the Alleghany mountains to the Kanawha, and thence to the Ohio River. Here again, Indian trails followed the streams or took short cuts and made use of the waterways at convenient places where a mountain was cut by a river and thus opened a way of least resistance. The gaps and Indian trails above mentioned are sufficient to illustrate the principle under consideration. In any study of the Virginia Frontier, the Potomac and the James routes are the ones that concern that frontier particularly.

It is evident that in the days of early settlement a river had importance in proportion to two things, namely, the extent of its penetration into an undiscovered, or at least unoccupied, country, and the distance it was navigable for boats of trade. Fur trading was, of course, an industry which at once attracted the quick eye of men of enterprise. Furs were secured from the Indians in exchange for trinkets of small value and if they could be conveniently carried to the Atlantic Coast there was a ready market for them,—if the owners did not elect themselves to supervise the sending of these desirable skins to Europe. If a river admitted of small trading boats being borne upon it (without obstacles in the way of falls) for a great distance, that river naturally became a highway for fur traffic. If an obstacle in the way of a considerable fall in the river stopped navigation, at that point it was natural to make a settlement. Thus, Richmond is at the falls of the James and Alexandria is at the falls of the Potomac.

But a river extending into forest country possessed dangers in time of war for the inhabitants of the sparsely settled country. The Hudson, with its great length of navigable waters was a menace as well as a source of revenue to the early settlers of that region. When, on the other hand, the Indians were once driven from the tidewater country of what is now eastern Virginia, there was no danger of savages floating down upon the coastal inhabitants by way of the Potomac or the James. The bearing which the topography of the Atlantic coast regions of the country had upon the movement of frontiersmen, Indians, and armies, has been so fully described [4] that there is no need to do more than give a few concrete illustrations. The Potomac-Alleghany route to the West prompted the Ohio Company to launch its land project and led westward to its particular region of operation. The Ohio Company's operations occasioned the French and Indian War. The first attempts to reach the French in the Ohio section by an embassy and later by an armed force, was through the use of this roadway of nature to the western country. It was finally Braddock's route. The route now followed by the Chesapeake and Ohio Railway to the western country, through what is now Staunton, Virginia, serves to show on its face how Augusta County, even as it now is, would be threatened by Indian invasions in times when colonial forces were diverted to other parts, or when the entire Virginia Frontier was weakened as it was after the defeat of Braddock. The same is true of the waterways of the James, the New, and the Kanawha rivers. The outlet to the West would naturally, in danger times, become the inlet from the back country for Indian invasion.

The easier and safer the route to the West, the more it would be traveled. Hence in early days questions arose as to what Indian tribes would be met in a proposed movement to the western frontier. When we speak of the tide of emigration from the eastern coast towards the western country, other elements, economic, political, or religious, play their part. But topography pointed the way that these

---

[4] E. C. Semple, American History and Its Geographic Conditions. See especially chapters ii-v.

human tides would flow, no matter what the cause of the flow.

By the year 1750, the North Carolina frontier had been pushed westward a hundred miles on the Cape Fear River, and along the Tar and Neuse Rivers to about where Hillsborough, North Carolina, now stands. The Virginia settlements had by this time passed the "Fall line" and reached the Blue Ridge Mountains. This was the natural westward advance of the "tidewater" population. The Blue Ridge Mountains served temporarily to check the westward advance of the tidewater people, but the fertile valley of the Shenandoah, just beyond, had for over a decade been filling rapidly with so-called "foreigners." These non-English people were, for the most part, Scotch-Irish[5] and Germans[6] that had come south from Pennsylvania by following the north-south valleys along the Alleghany and Blue Ridge Mountains. The southern part, or "upper" valley of the Shenandoah was taken up by the Scotch-Irish, while the northern, or "lower" valley, was settled by the Germans. The more daring Scotch-Irish had also taken advantage of the Potomac River passageway to press westward as far as Wills Creek. Settlements also extended along the South Branch of the Potomac to where Romney, Petersburg, and Franklin, West Virginia, now stand. In Pennsylvania these two elements in our early civilization had pushed as far as the present Berks and Lancaster counties—the Scotch-Irish farther out on the border than the more peaceable Germans. In part, because of the barrier formed by the Alleghany and Cumberland Mountains, these Pennsylvania settlers were readily deflected southward. A few of them stopped in Maryland, many of them in Virginia, and some drifted on to the Carolinas. The chief reason, however, for the migration from Pennsylvania southward was the intolerable conditions

---

[5] H. J. Ford, The Scotch-Irish in America; S. S. Green, The Scotch-Irish in America.
[6] Oscar Kuhns, The German and Swiss Settlements of Colonial Pennsylvania; J. W. Wayland, The German Element of the Shenandoah Valley of Virginia.

on the Pennsylvania frontier, where the country was without defenses of any kind because of the position taken on the matter of colonial defense by the Quaker lawmakers at Philadelphia.[7]

In New York, at this time, the most extreme western settlements had not passed beyond the head waters of the Delaware, except in the case of the Mohawk Valley. Here the land had been taken up almost to the very source of the river only about fifty miles from the English post at Oswego. The whole Atlantic coast frontier line was as uneven and tortuous as can be well imagined, resembling a huge hand spread out along the Atlantic coast—the base of the hand resting on the coast, with the fingers, represented by the numerous rivers, pointing westward and northwestward. The American home-seekers who wrestled with nature and with Indians had stuck close to the streams that penetrated the interior, chiefly for economic reasons, as streams afforded practically the only east-west means of transportation in colonial days. The lands between the rivers were occupied only after the best lands along the streams had been appropriated, and after a growth of population made their occupation a necessity.

The topographical background of our study, including the Indian trails and the brief reference to the drift of population westward, at once suggests that the immense tract of country west of the Appalachian range was bound to be a bone of contention between the two nations that claimed it. The people of the Atlantic slopes were the sort of people that would fit into the plan of nature such as was here presented. The avenues of approach to the western country were prepared by nature and the Indian,—nature's forest child. To all this may be added that the time was ripe for action. A struggle for the continent was at hand.

---

[7] W. T. Root, The Relations of Pennsylvania with the British Government, 1696-1765, p. 310, and passim.

CHAPTER III

Governor Dinwiddie and the Assembly

The events of 1753-1763 in American colonial history are pictured upon a European background. They are colored, however, by the racial, religious, and governmental conditions of the various colonies involved. The period covered by the French and Indian War in America was the period of the Georges in English history. Green has said of George I and of George II: "Their character as nearly approached insignificance as it is impossible for human character to approach it." He further says of George III: "He had a smaller mind than any English king before James II." While, however, there was no strength on the throne of England in these days, the times were made memorable because of Englishmen in both state and church who guided the affairs of the English people. These were the days of Clive in India, of William Pitt, who became in reality, though not in name, head of the British ministry, and of John Wesley, who was just inaugurating his apostolic work for England and the New World as well. In the earlier part of the struggle in America for English supremacy over the French, Pitt had not yet come to his own; but he took the oath of office in time to show his strong hand in bringing to a victorious end the war which was to decide whether America was to be dominantly English or French. Pitt said, upon assuming the high task of guiding England's destinies: "I want to call England out of that enervate state in which twenty thousand men from France can shake her." [1] The great statesman was right in feeling that there was need to "shake" somebody; but it was leadership that had been "enervate."

The hesitation and positive incompetence of the mother country in the earlier years of the French and Indian War

---

[1] J. R. Green, A Short History of the English People, pp. 721, 749, 761.

had been paralleled in America by absence of cooperation among the colonies. Hesitation characterized some of them; in others there were bickerings, and even conflicts between colony and colony, and also between the governors and their respective legislative assemblies. The defeat of Braddock was indeed a blessing in disguise, as it served to arouse the colonies to something of concerted action. But even then there was apathy in certain colonies that, as now seen in perspective, calls for explanation.

Nearly one hundred and fifty years had passed since the founding of Jamestown, Virginia. In the meantime New England had been settled by a religious contingent from English stock whose primary aim in coming to America was to have "a State without a king and a Church without a bishop." The Puritans were Nonconformists, but not necessarily Separatists. Their position was something like the attitude of John Wesley and his followers to the Established Church—"in it but not of it." Of course, the Puritans went farther than the Methodists in their attitude and practices so far as the Church of England was concerned. But both of these church folk found that on coming to America non-conformity to the Established Church became separatism in spirit and practice. At any rate, by the middle of the eighteenth century, the period of which we write, New England had become dominantly Congregational. The original Plymouth colony that had fled to America because of persecution for their religion, had developed into an intolerant state church, and then back to toleration of a cautious type. In the meantime, religion was the leading topic about which New Englanders wrote and spoke. At the very beginning of the period of the French and Indian War, when Robert Dinwiddie was appointed Governor of Virginia, Jonathan Edwards, the leading New England divine, was concerned only over the new appointee's religious status, saying [2] in a letter to a friend at the time, that Dinwiddie was a

---

[2] Charles Campbell, History of the Colony and Ancient Dominion of Virginia, p. 454.

Scotchman and had been reared up under the influence of the Presbyterian church, and would, as a consequence, have " respect for that church." This is a straw that tells which way the wind was blowing.

No characterization of the New England church at the time of the French and Indian War would be complete without some reference to the attitude of the people of that section to Roman Catholicism.[3] To them the French people, who had strongly entrenched themselves just to the north in what is now Canada, as well as to the west towards the Great Lakes region, were " Papists." It is not going too far to say that this term had about the same effect upon the earlier New Englander that the word " fire " would produce on persons living in the vicinity of a powder mill. When we search for motive or for impulse that inspired the people of New England to be more ready to fly at the French or their Indian allies than were their fellow-colonists, we find reason enough in this deep-seated feeling against " papists " and " popery." The fathers of the Congregationalists had taught their children that all the ills which they had suffered came of " popery" in spirit if not in fact. They had declared that only so far as the Church of England had become imbued with the spirit of Roman Catholicism was it a persecuting church. This condition in New England must be duly considered in order to comprehend the part that creed played in the attitude of the New England colonists in the French and Indian War. The hesitation to come to England's assistance because of the Established Church which the New Englander opposed was more than overruled by the alacrity with which they marshalled forces to fight " papists."

When we come to the consideration of New Netherland,

---

[3] Laws of New York, 1691-1718, p. 41; Massachusetts Province Laws, vol. i, p. 423; as early as 1670, Roger Williams, the famous New England preacher, had declared, "the French and Roman Jesuits, the firebrands of the world, for their godbelly sake, are kindling at our back in this country their hellish fires with all the natives of this country" (Quoted by C. J. H. Hayes, A Political and Social History of Modern Europe, vol. i, p. 307).

now become New York under English dominion, we find that here both race and creed combined to produce an indisposition to come to the help of England in a united effort to drive the French from the Ohio and Mississippi Valleys. While New York was English in name, it was at this time a cosmopolitan colony of many races and creeds. It has been said that as many as eighteen languages were spoken in the New York Colony at the time of which we write. The Dutch were there in full force, of course; but so were the Quakers of different nations. When we find the New York assembly hesitating to come to the aid of England in an attempt to drive the French from a fort (which the latter had built on the Ohio) on the basis, as the assembly said, that it was not clear to them that the French had made any encroachments upon "his majesty's dominions," [4] we may be pardoned for looking deeper than this excuse for the cause of such indifference to English supremacy. Cosmopolitan New York had not yet come to be the homogeneous New York of later years.

New Jersey [5] was at this time what might be called a slice of New York. In race and creed that colony was much like its neighbor, and, indeed, for some time the two had been administered by one governor. Maryland was, in spite of reports to the contrary, Roman Catholic in its dominant people, although the Protestants outstripped them numerically. Virginia was strongly for the Established Church of England, and at times intolerantly so. North Carolina was at this time in the throes of a conflict between the Establishment, to which the colony had originally adhered, and the spirit of dissent that now was rampant.[6]   South

---

[4] Minutes of the Provincial Council, Pennsylvania Colonial Records, vol. v, p. 748; W. C. Ford, Writings of Washington, vol. i, p. 40.

[5] Dinwiddie to Governor Jonathan Belcher of New Jersey, Nov. 8, 1754, in Dinwiddie Papers, vol. i, p. 392; ibid., Jan. 14, 1755, pp. 457-458; Dinwiddie to Lords of Trade, ibid., p. 279; see Appendix II, No. 8.

[6] S. B. Weeks, "The Religious Development in the Province of North Carolina," in The Johns Hopkins University Studies in His-

Carolina was ever disposed to "gang its ain gait," secure in its remoteness from northern enemies and supposedly at peace with its own Indian neighbors. The Church of England was strong in this colony but independency was also on the ground. According to Governor Glen's characterization of the South Carolina assembly,[7] that colony had begun very early to think and act for itself. It can thus be seen at a glance that there was little hope for cohesion or cooperation among the colonists on the basis of creed. And as creed and race were intermingled in early colonial life, we may speak of both these forces as deterrents to united effort in behalf of England's honor where the individual colony did not consider itself in any special danger from French and Indian depredations.

In connection with creeds as a cause of lack of cohesion in American colonial life at the time of the French and Indian War, special mention should be made of Pennsylvania and Maryland,[8] both of which were in the meshes of proprietary governments. These colonies were obliged to serve two masters. As a consequence, they served neither. Amidst the clash of people versus proprietor and king in these two colonies, the interests of the colonies as a whole were overlooked. Religious matters had played an important part in the founding of both Pennsylvania and Maryland. The Quakers, in these early days, though never a persecuting sect, found themselves at odds with every one else (the In-

---

torical and Political Science, vol. x, p. 277; E. I. McCormac, "Colonial Opposition to Authority," in University of California Publications in History, vol. i, No. 1, p. 87; see below, pp. 169-170.

[7] Glen to the Duke of Newcastle. "The people have the whole of the administration in their hands, and the governor, and thereby the crown, is stripped of its power" (quoted by E. M. Avery, History of the United States, vol. iv, p. 23).

[8] Dinwiddie to Lord Halifax, November 16, 1754, says that South Carolina, Pennsylvania, and the Jerseys have granted no supplies; that in Pennsylvania this is due to the presence of so many Germans, among whom are many "roman Catholicks, as also in m'yl'd, that I dread if the Fr. sh'd be permitted to make a Settlem't on the rich Lands of the Ohio, that by sending Invitations to them, from their religious Principles, they may be prevailed to go on to the Ohio and join the Fr. in Expectat'n of large Grants of Land" (Dinwiddie Papers, vol. i, p. 406; see Appendix II, No. 8).

dians excepted), and every one else at odds with them.   As
the Quakers[9] were almost all-powerful in Pennsylvania, the
fact that the creed of the dominant people of this colony
negatived the creed of every other religious sect, was cause
enough for want of cooperation with the other colonies.   But
when we add to this deterrent the other which grew out of
the refusal of the proprietor of the colony to allow his own
land to be taxed for means to defend it, we may well hesi-
tate to be over-harsh with the Pennsylvania assembly for
refusing to act with the other colonies until the parsimonious
Penns of England had agreed to take a hand in providing
means for colonial defense.   What is said of Pennsylvania
so far as proprietary government[10] is concerned was equally
true of Maryland.[11]   It seems to have been a toss-up between
the Penns and Frederick, Lord Baltimore, which of the two
should be the more parsimonious.

Another reason for the lack of cooperation between the
several colonies in the French and Indian War was the
absence of sympathy between the governors and the assemblies over which they presided.[12]   These governors were
appointed by the Crown, and were generally only lieutenant
or sub-governors, the titular governor living in England
while his representative presided over the colony as his deputy.
In some instances the governors got on well with their respective assemblies so long as little was asked of the people, but
we shall see later how Governor Dinwiddie almost wrecked
his popularity and the king's cause in the Virginia colony
by making a demand which the Virginia assembly resented.
Governor Sharpe, of Maryland, seems to have been an able

---

[9] C. J. Stille, " The Attitude of the Quakers in the Provincial
Wars," in Pennsylvania Magazine of History and Biography, vol.
x, pp. 283-319; Root, chap. xi; Isaac Sharpless, A Quaker Experi-
ment in Government, pp. 223-224.

[10] Dinwiddie Papers, vol. ii, pp. 46, 51, 60, 115, 181; see below,
pp. 172-173.

[11] The Maryland-Virginia boundary line question had also been
a matter of concern between Virginia and her northern neighbor
(Governor Sharpe to Lord Fairfax, Archives of Maryland, vol. vi,
p. 6; Lord Fairfax to Governor Sharpe. Sept. 24, 1753, ibid., p. 7;
Sharpe to Cecilius Calvert, June 6, 1754, ibid., pp. 69-71).

[12] McCormac, vol. i, No. 1, p. 1 ff.

official, loyal to the king and to his proprietors, and desirous [13]
of doing all he could to join the other colonies in an attempt
to defend the English claims in America against what was
thought to be French aggression. But the Maryland assembly
persisted in adding riders to otherwise excellent bills providing
for men and means for defense—those riders invariably having teeth for the proprietor of the colony and serving to
nullify these bills because Governor Sharpe felt that he
must sustain the man whom he represented in the colony.
The case of Governor Glen, of South Carolina, illustrates a
somewhat hopeless situation.[14] After all has been said, the
strength of Governor Dinwiddie is made the more apparent
when we note how he overcame opposition from one of the
most sullen and determined of colonial assemblies, and by
Scotch persistence finally made friends out of his very foes.
Dinwiddie built wiser than he knew for the future United
States.

Not only were the assemblies of the colonies disposed to
be independent and often positively defiant, but on the
extreme frontier we find a certain element or factor which
made against colonial cohesion. This factor was created in
part by national or racial peculiarities and in part by the
environment of the frontiersmen. While the inhabitants
along the Atlantic Coast and other sections from which the
Indians had long since been driven and which had become
established communities, were disposed to stress community

---

[13] Dinwiddie Papers, vol. i, pp. 67, 213, 424-429; vol. ii, pp. 127,
367-368; Forbes to Horatio Sharpe (Governor of Maryland from
August 10, 1753 to 1769), July 20, 1758, Archives of Maryland,
vol. xxxi, pp. 293-294; see Sharpe's speech to the Cherokees in 1755
(S. M. Hamilton, Letters to Washington, vol. i, pp. 61-63); J. T.
Scarf, History of Maryland, vol. i, pp. 243-244; see below, pp. 168-
169.

[14] See, for instance, Dinwiddie's scathing letter to James Glen
(Governor of South Carolina from 1744-1755, succeeded by William
Henry Lyttleton, 1755-1760), August 5, 1754, Dinwiddie Papers,
vol. i, pp. 272-276. Major Andrew Lewis wrote Governor Dinwiddie,
July 23, 1756, that the Cherokees "told me the Carolina People had
promis'd them from Time to Time to build them a Fort, but always
deceived them, for their Parts they had no Dependence on them
neither wou'd they believe their Coming 'till they see them . . ."
(Contemporary copy in Loudoun Papers, Lewis file, 1756).

and inter-colonial life, the frontiersmen on the very borders of the western rim of English possessions were very individualistic. This was what might naturally be expected. Men who are adventurous enough to live where they must in a moment's notice meet single-handed the savage of the American forest, would in the very nature of the case be men who had confidence in themselves. This confidence on the part of a man to take care of himself and family on a savage frontier develops individuality beyond anything of which we can conceive in our day. If to this frontier environment we add Scotch-Irish hardihood and tenacity, we have a combination which might suggest the Scotch Highlanders of Scott's romances. The colonial frontiersman of the French and Indian War period was a law unto himself. If he could be induced to fight for a colony or a confederacy of colonies, he became a force that the foe had to reckon with; but he was not easily induced to be communal enough to fight for rights which were clouded in disputes about " discovery claims." Thus a study of the Virginia Frontier calls for an understanding of the pioneer spirit as well as a knowledge of conditions in England and in the several colonies under English jurisdiction in America. With these general conditions in view we may turn to Governor Dinwiddie and the Virginia popular body, the House of Burgesses.

Robert Dinwiddie,[15] who occupied the office of lieutenant-governor in the Virginia colony from 1751 to 1758, was born in Scotland in 1693. In 1727 he was appointed collector of customs in the island of Bermuda. For his vigilance in detecting a fraud in the system in use there, he was appointed in 1738 " Surveyor-General of Customs of the south-

---

[15] The Dinwiddie Papers, with an introduction by R. A. Brock, are published in the Virginia Historical Society Collections, n. s., vols. iii and iv. Dinwiddie was only the lieutenant governor. The governor at this time was the Earl of Albemarle who succeeded to the sinecure in 1737. Albemarle died in 1754 and was followed by John Campbell, Earl of Loudoun, who was governor in chief from 1756 to 1763. Like most of the sinecure holders he resided in London. The title " governor " is usually given the lieutenant governors.

ern ports of the Continent of America." He seems to have lived in London in 1749, engaged in trade with the American colonies. He was commissioned lieutenant-governor of Virginia July 20, 1751. He arrived in Virginia, November 20, of that year. The first patents signed by Dinwiddie bear the date of April 28, 1752. His first meeting [16] with the assembly was on February 27, 1752.

Dinwiddie's first address to his assembly indicates how clearly he comprehended the entire colonial situation, not only as it affected Virginia, but England. The governor was ever disposed to think of the colony over which he presided as a means to accomplish an end much above the mere good of the colony itself. With rare foresight and statesmanship, Dinwiddie saw both the strength and weakness of the English situation in America. In his first address, after bestowing many fulsome compliments upon the Virginians, and assuring them among other things, that it would be his " constant care to support the Church of England, as by law established," [17] he brought forward as one of the matters of first importance the relations of the colony to the Indians. The governor said:

I recommend to your particular Regard the Cultivating a good Correspondence with the Neighboring Nations of *Indians*. It is better they should love us, than that they should fear us; and one of the Two is absolutely necessary. Fear is a slavish Passion, and the Mind is always struggling to throw it off. On the contrary, Love and Amity are propagated by Acts of Kindness. . . . Our European Neighbors, who are settled to the Southward and

---

[16] The first session lasted from February 27 to April 20, 1752.

[17] Journals of the House of Burgesses, 1752-1758, p. 4. Later references will be entitled " Journal." The appointive council and the elective house of burgesses (see Appendix II, Dinwiddie's Report to the Lords Commissioners) made up the General Assembly; however, writers commonly use, as has been done in this study, the term assembly as synonymous with house of burgesses. Brock says of Dinwiddie: " It should not be forgotten that . . . he was a warm friend of religion, and, withal, entirely tolerant of all mere differences of creed; that he sought the enforcement of morality, and was the patron of knowledge and education" (Dinwiddie Papers, vol. i, p. xiii; see Dinwiddie's letter to Major Andrew Lewis, April 24, 1756, ibid., vol. ii, p. 390). It is interesting to note that drama made its first appearance in America at the Williamsburg Theater, under the patronage of Governor Dinwiddie, September 5, 1752.

Northward of us, would never be able to inflame the *Indians* against us, if the Advantage of mutual Bounty, Gratitude, and public Faith, opposed Attempts. They have long been endeavoring to spirit us the *Indians* that are in Amity with us, to the Breach of their Faith, with a view to possess, and settle the interior Parts of *America,* the Back of our Frontier Settlements to the Westward. Your own good Sense will soon discover, what bad Consequences such Settlements would be to us, and our Posterity.[18]

It is evident that while addressing the Virginia assembly Dinwiddie had in view the whole colonial situation. He saw that the French to the north and the Spaniards to the south would use the Indians as agents to drive the English from the American continent. The French and Indian War was a cloud on the horizon, not larger than a man's hand, probably, but nevertheless a cloud—and it meant the coming storm.

The governor also in his first address suggested that means be devised by the assembly to prevent delays in courts of justice.[19] As this was named first in order of recommendations, the assembly at once set to work to comply with the request. While they were doing this the governor announced that the king had repealed ten acts passed by the preceding assembly. This put a stop to action in the direction of lawmaking to prevent delays in justice, but it did not, it seems, interfere with the cordial feelings which the assembly felt and expressed for the governor. Indeed, the assembly at once took up the entire matter of relations with the Indians, and, among other things, passed an act " for encouraging persons to settle on the waters of the Mississippi in the county of Augusta." [20] This act looked to encouraging peace with the Indians by having settlers from the Virginia colony live among them. It also had reference to speeding up the already notable emigration to western lands.

As an indirect means of promoting peaceful relations with the Indians, the Virginia assembly had long considered set-

---

[18] Journals, p. 5.
[19] Ibid.
[20] W. W. Hening, Statutes at Large, vol. vi, p. 258; Journals, pp. 68, 70, 72, 76, 83, 98.

ting up strong buffer colonies [21] to serve as outposts against
the French.   This explains, as McIlwaine observes, the settlement of the Huguenots at Manakin Town, the Germans at
Germanna, and the hearty welcome extended to the Scotch-
Irish and the Germans in the Valley of Virginia.[22]   With
the French now become a real menace on the border, the
need for such outlying settlements [23] was felt more keenly
than ever.   Even the denominational bars were let down
and such settlers " being Protestants " were exempted from
the " payment of all public, county, and parish levies for a
term of ten years." [24]

As a testimony of goodwill towards the new governor,
the assembly at the close of its first session voted him as a
present the sum of £500, a complete refutation of the idea
that Dinwiddie was from the first unpopular with the Virginia people.[25]

The second [26] session of the Virginia assembly under Governor Dinwiddie was called at the command of the king " to
lay before them the Necessity of a mutual Assistance, and
to engage them to grant such Supplies, as the Exigency of
the present Affairs requires . . . for defeating the Designs
of our Enemies." [27]   The French " designs " had so far
taken form that they had already erected a fort in the Ohio
region and were preparing to build others at important
points.   Dinwiddie told the assembly that he had " been
alarmed by several Informations from our Back Settlements,
from the Indians, and from our Neighbouring Governors "
of the approach of the French and their Indian allies towards

[21] A scheme in 1730 for settling Palatines on the Ohio had been
frustrated (Draper, MSS., 1B120).
[22] Journals, pp. xiii-xiv.
[23] For considerable matter, with references, on the western movement, see Draper, MSS., 1B156-183; Samuel Kercheval, History of
the Valley, pp. 41-50.
[24] Hening, vol. vi, p. 258.
[25] Journals, pp. xv n., xxvii; Campbell, p. 455; A. G. Bradley, The
Fight with France for North America, p. 57; Doyle, vol. v, p. 429;
Jared Sparks, Writings of Washington, vol. i, p. 90.
[26] From Nov. 1-Dec. 19, 1753.
[27] Journals, p. 104.

the Ohio, and that he had by the advice of the council " sent several considerable Presents to the Indians, that are our Allies, and in Friendship with us." He also said: " I intend to meet the Chiefs of the different Tribes of Indians, next May, at Winchester, to deliver a very considerable Present from his Majesty; I am in great hopes then, to make a firm, strong, and lasting Alliance with them." [28]

The governor advised the assembly that the " Attempt of the French has been represented to the Ministry at Home, by several Governors on this Continent, and by myself; and by them (the Ministry at Home) it was laid before the King." [29] Furthermore, " His Majesty out of his paternal Love, Affection, and great Regard he bears to his Subjects on this Continent, immediately ordered one of his Ships of War to come to this Dominion, with Royal Instructions to me, how to conduct myself, in the present Situation of Affairs; I also received Letters to all his Majesty's Governors on this Continent with Orders to dispatch the Same to them immediately." [30] From these communications it may be assumed that Dinwiddie's capacity and loyalty were appreciated in England, and that the Government in this affair at least was making use of the Virginia executive to get the king's wishes to other governors.

The second important recommendation of Governor Dinwiddie to this session of the assembly concerned the militia. In his own peculiar way he said:

As I am of the Opinion, That the Militia Law is deficient in some Points, I shall lay before you some Remarks thereon for your Consideration; As our Militia, under God, is our chief Dependence, for the Protection of your Lives and Fortunes; (our Country being very extensive and without fortifications), I doubt not you will think it a proper Step to look into that Law, and make such Alteration and Amendment as to you may be thought necessary.[31]

In the above recommendation there was not only sound advice, but the nucleus of one of the most statesmanlike enterprises of Governor Dinwiddie's administration, namely,

[28] Ibid., p. 104.
[29] Ibid., p. 104.
[30] Ibid., p. 104.
[31] Ibid., p. 105.

the fortification of the entire Virginia Frontier. It will be seen later how this was accomplished.[32]

At the same time two distinct elements made for discord in this second assembly. The first of these was a complaint from the home government concerning the bad quality of the tobacco which the colony had sent to England. Dinwiddie said: "I conceive this must be greatly owing to the Neglect and Dishonesty of the Inspectors: I therefore recommend to your Consideration, whether the Reduction of the vast Number of the Warehouses, and the appointing an Inspector-General in each River, properly impowered to inspect the different Warehouses, and to examine the Books of the Inspectors, would not be of Service to remove the Complaints now subsisting."[33] Anything that affected the tobacco trade in Virginia at this time touched a vital nerve in the life of the colony, consequently most of the time of the assembly was taken up in discussing the pros and cons of the tobacco situation and little attention was paid to the protection of the frontier.

The other cause of discord concerned what was known as the "pistole fee" dispute. The facts seem to be as follows: When Dinwiddie was appointed governor of Virginia there were in the secretary's office as many as a thousand patents made out ready to be passed under the seal. There were as many more surveyor's certificates for land in connection with which all preliminary steps had already been taken, awaiting the issuing of the patents. Dinwiddie's quick business eye saw in the situation a chance to make a few hundred pounds by attaching a small fee to every patent that might pass under his seal.[34] Technically, the governor had a right to exact this fee. It was only 18 pence[35] in the case of each patent, and as the assembly had been generous enough to

---

[32] See chap. vi.
[33] Journals, p. 103.
[34] Ibid., pp. xvi-xviii.
[35] About $3.50 (Doyle, vol. v, p. 433, referring to Crosby, Early Coins in America, p. 116); Brock says the value was $3.60 (Dinwiddie Papers, vol. i, p. 44).

present the governor with £500 as a present at the close of the first session, probably the governor reasoned that generosity like this would not find fault with the small fee that he was demanding, which, like a notary's fee, was given for the setting of his seal upon a patent. What was $3.50 to a man who would, on paying it, get his " grant " of land legally secured! But Dinwiddie reasoned without his host. Never before, probably, did so small a matter create so great a storm in an assembly.[36] The burgesses made quick calculation. They figured on the one thousand or more patents that were now awaiting the executive's signature—patents which Dinwiddie had had nothing whatever to do with, but that came to him as a lucky inheritance either from past oversight or because the colony had not had a governor for two years. This sum of between three and four thousand dollars was, as the assembly thought, "easy money," and they resented the new governor's taking advantage of his situation to collect it from the colonists. To add to the governor's offense he had kept the pistole fee proposal up his sleeve during the entire session and announced it only at the close. The assembly vowed it had been hoodwinked and that their governor's only interest in the colony came from his desire for personal gain. The resentment was so hot that this one act of Governor Dinwiddie's dogged his administration throughout the entire life of the assembly of 1752-1755. It occasioned a visit of Peyton Randolph to England in behalf of the assembly and thus came perilously near injuring the governor in the estimation of the home government. Dinwiddie eventually saw that his action had been tactless, even though he could have justified himself technically. In a letter written to James Abercromby,[37]

---

[36] Journals, pp. 129-168; Dinwiddie Papers, vol. i, pp. 72, 370-375.
[37] Dinwiddie Papers, vol. i, p. 137. The titular governor, holder of the sinecure, received £1,665 of the £2,000 regular salary paid from the revenue arising from the 2s. per hogshead tax on tobacco exported. The lieutenant governor was, however, able to add in various ways to the part coming to him, so that, according to McIlwaine, it is safe to say he was a well paid officer (H. R. Mc-Ilwaine, Journals, 1752-1755, p. xiii).

the colony's agent in London, April 26, 1754, he confessed: "If I had known that this Affair would have created so much Uneasiness to me and Trouble to my Friends at Home, I would not have taken that Fee."

This pistole fee episode is referred to here at length because of the part it played in controlling the action of the assembly in regard to anything which Governor Dinwiddie afterwards recommended. He had positively alienated for the time, the Virginia assembly, had created suspicion in their minds concerning his sincerity, and as a consequence we find at the most critical period yet reached in the history of American colonial affairs, the governor and assembly of the most prominent of the colonies hopelessly at odds with each other over a matter of slight importance.

A reflex effect of the pistole episode upon the rank and file of the Virginia frontiersmen, who should have been in a position to support the governor cordially, is to be seen in a petition from the county but lately named in honor of the governor himself. In this address there is shadowed the position which the colonists would finally take on questions which concerned their "life, liberty, and sacred honor." The address from Dinwiddie County reads as follows:

We do humbly, but in the strongest Terms, represent to your Honour, that it is the undoubted Right of the Burgesses to enquire into the Grievances of the People: They have constantly exercised this Right, and we presume to affirm, that the drawing it into Question, in any Manner, cannot but be dangerous Consequence to the Liberties of his Majesty's faithful Subjects, and to the Constitution of this Government. The Rights of the Subjects are secured by Law, that they cannot be deprived of the least Part of their Property, but by their own Consent: Upon this excellent Principle is our Constitution founded, and ever since this Colony has had the Happiness of being under the immediate Protection of the Crown, the Royal Declarations have been, "That no Man's Life, Member, Household or Goods, be taken away or harmed, but by established and known Laws." [38]

The third session of the Virginia assembly which was called February 14, 1754, was hurriedly convened to hear an important piece of information. This information was

---

[38] Journals, p. 143.

nothing less than a report from the youthful George Washington who had already been sent to the extreme frontier of Virginia to bear a message to the French commander who had built a fort upon what was claimed to be Virginia territory. To apprehend the bearings of this report it is necessary to recall a series of events which had taken place during the previous six years.

In the year 1748 a corporation was formed known as the Ohio Company,[39] which was composed of prominent Virginia colonists and a few Londoners. This corporation was granted a tract of five hundred thousand acres on the Ohio River. In 1750 Christopher Gist had been employed by the company to survey the land, and his reports,[40] returned in October, 1752, were so satisfactory that the company hastened to carry out the provisions of the contract whereby they were to erect suitable forts in the region to be opened up.

This act on the part of the Ohio Company aroused the

---

[39] B. Fernow, Ohio Valley in Colonial Times, pp. 240-273; the Greenbrier Land Company was granted 100,000 acres on the Greenbrier River (ibid., p. 89). The Ohio Company was formed in 1748 by Thomas Lee and twelve others, including Lawrence and Augustine, brothers of George Washington in Virginia, and John Hanbury, a Quaker merchant of London, with a grant of 500,000 acres of land on the Ohio, between the Monongahela and Kanawha Rivers, chiefly on the north, but with the privilege of lands on the south side of the river. Two hundred thousand acres of land were to be settled immediately, to be free from quit-rents or other tax to the king, on condition that the Company should at their own expense send 100 families on the lands within seven years, build a fort and maintain a garrison sufficient to protect the settlement. The troubles with the French and Indians suspended the operations of the company until the close of the war. Lee dying, Lawrence Washington succeeded to the chief management of the company, and by purchase Governor Dinwiddie and George Mason became owners of shares in it (R. A. Brock, Dinwiddie Papers. vol. i, pp. 17-18 n.). Dinwiddie in 1754 issued a proclamation promising to lay out 200,000 acres of land adjacent to the fort at the Forks of the Ohio, then begun, which was to be divided among the soldiers who enlisted for service against the French. But Governor Hamilton of Pennsylvania demurred. Dinwiddie then agreed that the quit-rents of those lands might be collected by Pennsylvania until the dispute over the boundary line between Virginia and Pennsylvania was settled. He then applied to England to have the boundary line run. This was not done, however, until 1779; see below, pp. 60, 61.

[40] Christopher Gist's Journals, ed. by William M. Darlington.

French who had laid claim to this entire section. It is a well known fact that they had, about the time of the organization of the Ohio Company, placed along the Ohio River their famous leaden plates indicating that they claimed the region drained by that river. The French had secured communication between Lake Erie and the waters of the upper Ohio and had by mutual understanding and friendship with the Indians of that region, or through intimidation, gained valuable concessions from the natives. A fort at Presqu' Isle on Lake Erie (where the city of Erie now stands) and another at Le Boeuf (Waterford, Pennsylvania) twenty miles south had been built, but they had also seized the English trading post at Venango (site of Franklin, Pennsylvania). This was a positive step of agression. The next logical move would have been for the French to get control of the forks of the Ohio, and thus step by step make their way into the heart of the English possessions.

Dinwiddie had naturally become alarmed at what he had heard concerning French activities and had sent George Washington [41] as his ambassador both to inquire of the French commander concerning these acts and to warn him that he was on English territory. The reply of the French commander was evasive but sufficiently pointed to let Dinwiddie know that the French were there to stay. It was this disconcerting reply which Washington brought back to Dinwiddie and which was the occasion of the calling together hurriedly of the third session of the Virginia assembly.

But for the fact that the governor of the colony had rendered himself *persona non grata,* the assembly no doubt would have responded cordially to the very sane recommendation of the governor which was as follows:

I doubt not . . . but you will enable me by a full and sufficient Supply to exert the most Vigorous Efforts to secure the Rights and assert the Honour and Dignity of our Sovereign; to drive away these cruel and treacherous Invaders of your Property, and Destroyers of your Families, and thereby to gratify my warmest wishes

[41] Washington's Journal in Ford, Writings of Washington, vol. i, pp. 11-40.

in establishing the Security and Prosperity of Virginia, on the most solid and permanent Foundations.[42]

This appeal brought forth a miserable appropriation of ten thousand pounds sterling, which ridiculously small sum [43] voted at the third session for the defense of the colony must have made the governor inwardly curse the day that he irritated the Virginia burgesses. The assembly furthermore made a few changes in the law governing the militia, but these changes did not render that body sufficiently effective in the emergency that it was to confront.

An implied distrust of the governor, which very much offended him, is seen in an act[44] passed at the same session providing for directors who should from time to time, with the consent of the governor or commander-in-chief, direct and appoint how money that had been voted for defense should be applied toward the protecting and defending his majesty's subjects who were then settled, or who should thereafter settle, on the river Mississippi. It was now Dinwiddie's time vigorously to protest against this encroachment upon his rights as the king's representative, as he was entitled to have entire charge of the expenditure of money raised by the act. The governor was doubtless right, but his alienated and suspicious assembly had had their Virginia blood aroused and since money could be secured on no other terms, the governor was compelled to sign the bill with the unpalatable feature incorporated in it. How far Dinwiddie and his assembly had drifted apart is to be seen in a letter to the British Lords of Trade concerning the work of the third session, in which the governor declared that the only thing which kept him from dissolving the assembly was the hope of getting from England an order to dissolve it by proclamation and thus more severely rebuke them, than by merely doing it himself.[45]

To anticipate events, in order to dispose of the matter of

---

[42] Journals, p. 176.
[43] Ibid., p. xviii.
[44] Hening, vol. vi, p. 418; Dinwiddie Papers, vol. i, p. 98.
[45] Dinwiddie Papers, vol. i, p. 161.

Dinwiddie's conflicts with the Virginia assembly, the fourth session of that body which convened August 22, 1754, heard the alarming announcement of Washington's capitulation at Fort Necessity. The alarm of the assembly over the situation is shown in a bill which they drew up for the raising of £20,000 for the purposes of a campaign against French aggression. But the pistole fee, like Banquo's ghost, once more manifested itself. This time it took the form of adding a rider [46] to this otherwise satisfactory bill, asking for £2,500 to be paid to Peyton Randolph for his services to the assembly when he represented the matter of the pistole fee to the English court. The council of course rejected the bill, and had they not done so the governor surely would have withheld his signature. As a consequence, the assembly was prorogued [47] and its measures were thus rendered abortive. In the meantime, the situation on the frontier was not only alarming, but one that positively threatened disaster [48] to British interests in America. [49]

Attention has been called in a general way to the absence of cohesion in the colonies of America at the outbreak of the struggle between the British and the French for the lands west of the Alleghanies. The causes of a lack of cooperation have been referred to as racial, religious, and the political conflicts in the colonies between the popular bodies of the legislatures on the one hand and the governors and proprietors on the other. Specific reference has been made to Dinwiddie's difficulties with his assembly in the Virginia colony, but the story of his fight for British territory in the western country would not be complete without showing how

---

[46] Journals, p. 201; Dinwiddie Papers, vol. i, p. 324.

[47] Ibid., p. 205.

[48] For "A Register of Persons who have been either killed, wounded or taken Prisoners by the Enemy in Augusta, as also of such as have made their Escape," October, 1754-May, 1758, see Draper, MSS., 1QQ83.

[49] For an interesting brief summary of the military situation in Virginia from 1753-1756, see a letter from Colonial Richard Bland to ——. Upon the back of the manuscript copy is inscribed in Washington's handwriting, "Written It is supposed by Colo. Richard Bland 1756" (S. M. Hamilton, Letters to Washington, vol. i, pp. 386-395).

the aloofness of the other colonies discouraged the Virginia assembly and nearly broke the spirit of Virginia's governor.

From the mass of Dinwiddie's letters at this period it is necessary to open only a few at random to detect the note which runs through them all. We can not charge him with being a chronic complainer, as he was only too glad to give praise where praise could possibly be given. We are forced to the conclusion, therefore, that his letter to Governor Sharpe, June 20, 1754, contains in principle the truth: "It is cruel our neighboring Colonies are so backward in granting Supplies and I find I shall be much straitened for Money to furnish Provisions &c. I therefore still have a Dependence on some Assistance from your Province, being thorowly convinced of your hearty Inclinations." [50]

To Governor Hamilton of Pennsylvania, June 18, 1754, he wrote: "I am sorry your Assembly is so obstinate and disobedient to the royal Commands as I had a thorow dependence on You for a Supply of Bread, the want of which puts me in great difficulties." [51] Later he wrote to Governor Hamilton, under date of July 31: "It is most certain that if the neighboring Colonies had given due Assistance, the last unlucky Affair would not have happened; to the Contrary it's more than probable by this Time we should have forced the Enemy from the Ohio." [52] Dinwiddie is referring to the defeat of Washington's forces at Great Meadows when he is speaking of the "last unlucky affair." On the same date that he wrote Governor Hamilton, (July 31), he wrote to Governor DeLancey, of New York, candidly saying: "Their tedious delays (the coming of the New York troops) in coming here has given the French the advantage over us, which You may observe by the inclosed News Paper which is the true Report given by our officers. . . . If Your two

---

[50] Dinwiddie Papers, vol. i, p. 213.
[51] Ibid., p. 214.
[52] Ibid., p. 257. James Hamilton was Governor of Pennsylvania 1748-1754 and 1759-1768. Robert Hunter Morris was lieutenant-governor from October, 1754 to August, 1756.

Companies had come in Time, the French, in all probability, would not have attacked us." [53]

In writing to James Abercrombie, June 18, 1754, Dinwiddie stated in more general terms the indifference of two of the colonies adjacent to him: "Maryland and Pennsylvania, two proprietary Governments, do nothing tho' equally concerned and more exposed than this Dominion." [54] In the same connection a letter to the Earl of Albemarle, July 24, says: "I am now convinced this Expedition can not be conducted by any Dependence on our neighboring Colonies." [55] This "expedition" refers to the next move he was making to strike the French after Washington's capitulation. He was pleading for help from the home government. This came in the form of Braddock's regiments. Governor Dinwiddie was humiliated and exasperated by the occasion given the French to taunt the English and their Indian allies with the want of cohesion among the colonies and also about their "slow movements." On June 18, 1754, he wrote to Sir Thomas Robinson: "The French too justly observe the want of connection in the Colonies, and from thence conclude (as they declare without reserve) that although we are vastly superior to them in Numbers, that they can take and secure the Country before we can agree to hinder them." [56]

The situation so far as Governor Dinwiddie's difficulties are concerned may be thus summed up: At the beginning of the struggle with the French and Indians when he saw that

---

[53] Ibid., p. 259. James De Lancey was lieutenant governor of New York 1753-1755, and again from 1757-1760; Sir Charles Hardy was governor in the interim.

[54] Ibid., p. 211. The colony of Virginia appears to have been represented at the English court by an agent from 1680. At first there was a single agent; later, as jealousy developed between the two legislative branches—the governor and council on the one hand and the house of burgesses on the other—each employed an agent. Thus James Abercromby (also spelled Abercrombie) was the sole agent from January, 1753, to January, 1758 (when the burgesses appointed one Montague to represent them), and of the governor and council only, to March, 1773, and perhaps later (ibid., p. 37).

[55] Ibid., p. 248.

[56] Ibid., p. 203.

they were entrenching themselves and would, if not stopped
in time, be too strongly fortified to be driven off, he planned
and pleaded in vain for assistance from the neighboring
colonies.   Practically single-handed he attempted first by
using Trent, and later by an armed force under Washington,
to occupy the strategic point at the Forks of the Ohio.   The
failure of these attempts drove him almost frantic, not, as
we see in his letters, because of any reflection which the failure of these expeditions would cast upon him, but because
of his loyalty and zeal for the British cause.   The indifference
of the assemblies of the colonies and the hesitation of some
of the governors themselves, presented a situation utterly
incomprehensible to a man of Dinwiddie's type.   He was
aware that difference in creeds played no little part in the
lack of sympathy of some colonies with others.[57]   He knew
that the Germans in certain sections persisted in staying to
themselves and even refused to speak other than their language.[58]   He knew that most of the assemblies in the colonies
were disposed to give little heed to their Crown-appointed
governors.   He had himself suffered humiliation and almost
insult from his Virginia assembly, because its members
misunderstood his real nature, but, in the face of all this,
Dinwiddie did not lose faith in the final outcome.   Whatever

---

[57] Ibid., p. 406.

[58] "The Germans in Pennsyl'a live all in a Body together, as if
in a Principality of Germany, may they not in Time throw off
their Obedience and Submission to the B. Crown?   It was, I think,
a very imprudent Step in the first Settlem't of y't Province not to
mix them in their Settlem'ts with the Engl., and have English School
Masters, &c.   Whereas, there are now many Thousands cannot speak
one word of English" (ibid., p. 406).   The large number of slaves
in Virginia at this time added to the general anxiety and to the prob-
lem of adequate defense.   Dinwiddie reported to the Earl of Loudoun,
August 9, 1756, that the negro tithables in the colony were 60,078,
and the negro population, therefore, 120,156, and added, "Y's No.
of Negroes alarms our People much and are aff'd of bad Consequences if the Militia are order'd to any great Distance from the
pres't Settlem'ts" (ibid., vol. ii, p. 474; and see Appendix II, p. 168).
In Virginia slaves appear to have been employed at times for non-
combatant military duty.   Washington wrote to Captain Hog, December 27, 1755, "I think it will be advisable to detain both mulat-
toes & negroes in your company, and employ them as Pioneers or
Hatchetmen" (Ford, Writings of Washington, vol. i, p. 299 n.)

were the man's faults, or infirmities, candid opinion must pronounce him brave, loyal, resourceful, and indefatigable.[95] McIlwaine truly says in his introduction to the Journals of the House of Burgesses, 1756-58: " Dinwiddie's unremitting labors in behalf of Virginia in her period of trial were beginning to be appreciated and to a certain extent his ability in questions of finance.[60]

Dinwiddie's character has been written of hitherto largely upon certain assumptions, namely, that he was a Scotchman and untitled, hence could not make an appeal to prominent men of Virginia such as a man of Fauquier's stamp could; that Dinwiddie had formerly served Virginia in an office which would make any man unpopular with the people with whom he dealt in his official capacity; that Dinwiddie was almost miserly in his love of money; that he was untactful and haughty; that he was unpopular from the very start with the Virginia colony and continued to be so to the end.

Dinwiddie was certainly anything but unpopular with the Virginia assembly when he first appeared before them, and during the entire first session of the legislature. The utmost good will and even cordial feelings existed between the governor and the burgesses. The vote of £500 to the governor as a purse on the part of the burgesses at the close of the first session of the assembly indicates how unusual were the relations between the new appointee and the burgesses. Dinwiddie's attitude toward the Church and the Common Good were sincerely appreciated and reciprocated by the assembly. The occasion for alienation and even bitterness between the governor and the governing body in the colony developed in the second session of the assembly, as we have seen. Dinwiddie's course in the matter of the " pistole fee " is almost unaccountable in the light of his undoubted devotion to the interests of the colony and to the king of England.

---

[59] The remarkably comprehensive " Report from Governor Dinwiddie on the present state of Virginia. Transmitted the Lords Commissioners for Trade and Plantations, January, 1755," showing the governor's intimate acquaintance with the entire colonial situation, is given in full in Appendix II, No. 1.

[60] Journals, p. xxvii.

The real greatness of Dinwiddie is seen in this,—despite this unaccountable blunder at the very beginning of his administration, he was so persistent in his endeavors for the real good of the colony, so able in his advice and appointments of men, and came to be so respected by other governors of colonies for his untiring, self-sacrificing work for the cause both in and out of Virginia, that Dinwiddie came into his own before his administration ceased.   It may not take especial strength to hold popularity which good fortune gives to a man because of the position he happens to occupy to a governed body; but it takes a man of unusual ability and unselfishness to rise from the position of being as despised as Governor Dinwiddie was in the midst of the " pistole fee " episode, to where he was respected and almost revered for his services to the colony.

Dinwiddie saw with perfect clearness from the very day that he took the office of governor of the Virginia Colony where the stress should be laid in the colony's policies.   He hit the high points with an accuracy that is amazing.   He saw that the frontier was unfortified, and thus anticipated what he afterwards was largely instrumental in effecting. He saw that the militia would have to be the colony's dependence in lieu of a non-fortified border.   He saw that peace with the Indians would save many wars with them and that love was better than fear as a deterrent.

Of the two outstanding acts of Dinwiddie's in the interest of the Virginia colony, we would probably select his appointment of George Washington, first as ambassador to the French commander on the Ohio, which brought to the front this mere youth who was destined to have such a hand in shaping his country's future; then, in later giving Washington command of the entire colonial force.   In close connection with this selection of Washington as the outstanding figure in Virginia's colonial wars at this time, mention must be made of the determination of Dinwiddie to fortify the entire Virginia frontier.   This he did in close connection with, and with the cooperation of, Washington.   This act of Dinwiddie's can hardly be sufficiently appreciated. It served to inspire settlers to move west without hesitation; it discouraged the Indians from attempts upon the lives of the frontiersmen of Virginia and in fact upon making attacks upon the border at all. It had its influence in driving the main attacks of the French and Indians to the north where the strong hand of Pitt, who had by that time come to the ministry in England, gave the enemy the decisive blow at Quebec.

CHAPTER IV

WASHINGTON'S PART IN THE FRENCH AND INDIAN WAR

Reference has been made already to the selection of George Washington by Governor Dinwiddie to bear to the French Commander on the Ohio a message which, while courteous, was so explicit in its claims in behalf of the English people that the governor of the Virginia colony must have known that he committed himself to hostilities if the French commander rejected his demands. The choice of Washington on the part of Dinwiddie to be his ambassador on so important a mission will forever associate these two men in history. As the great American emerges here for the first time in connection with services in behalf of the country that he lived only to serve, this chapter is headed with his name. From this time until the crisis on the Virginia Frontier had passed he dominates the situation.

George Washington, at the time he acted as Dinwiddie's ambassador to the French commander on the Ohio, was only twenty-one years old. Having received his credentials [1] at Williamsburg, Virginia, October 31, 1753, and having also selected a French and an Indian interpreter, he promptly set out the same day upon his adventurous journey. The winter was at hand and Washington had before him a distance of five or six hundred miles through a region practically untrodden save by the Indians of the forest.

---

[1] Washington's Journal in Ford, Writings of Washington, vol. i, pp. 11-40; Gist's Journal is printed in the Collections of the Massachusetts Historical Society, Series III, vol. v, p. 102. The following distances to points in the section of warlike operations are given in the Virginia Almanac of 1756:

"Fort Cumberland, Wills's Creek from Williamsburg.. 259 miles
From Wills's Creek to Little Meadows, ... 20 miles
From Wills's Creek to Great Crossing of Yauyaugany,.. 20 miles
From Wills's Creek to Great Meadows, ... 12 miles
From Wills's Creek to Gist's Plantation, ... 12 miles
From Wills's Creek to 2d Crossing of Yauyaugany, ... 5 miles
From Wills's Creek to Fort Duquesne, ... 7 miles
From Wills's Creek to Frazier's, ... 40 miles"

(R. A. Brock, Dinwiddie Papers, vol. i, p. 169 n.).

49

4

Having passed through the towns of Fredericksburg, Alexandria, and Winchester, Washington reached Wills Creek on the 14th of November.   Here he found Christopher Gist whom he induced to accompany him on his journey.   In Gist, Washington secured a faithful guide and one familiar with the country.   The party now consisted of eight persons.   Provided with suitable horses, tents, equipment, and provisions, they proceeded.   Progress was slow.   The inclemency of the weather was against them, the heavy snows made passage over the mountains difficult, and the crossing of the valleys was rendered perilous by the swelling of the streams, so that getting over them on frail rafts, fording, or swimming consumed time and required patience.

Washington's route lay past Gist's new house near the Big Yough, and thirty miles further, John Frazier's, on the Monongahela, at the mouth of Turtle Creek.   The latter they reached on November 22.   Frazier was a trader whom the French had recently driven from Venango, an Indian trading post on the Allegheny at the point where French Creek joins it.   The French had promptly fortified this post and called it Fort Machault.   From Frazier's Washington pushed on to the " Forks " of the Ohio.   On this spot where the Ohio Company intended to build a fort and which Washington noted with so much pleasure, Shingiss, King of the Delawares, was found living.   Washington's military sense instinctively recognized that the location was of great strategic importance.   A fort at that place would, he said, " be well situated on the Ohio, and have the entire command of the Monongahela; which runs up to our Settlements and is extremely well designed for Water Carriage."

On December 25, Washington reached Logstown, about twenty miles below the " Forks," where he held one of his characteristic conferences with the Indians and showed that he knew how to make a telling Indian speech.

Brothers, I have called you together in Council by order of your Brother, the Governor of *Virginia*, to acquaint you, that I am sent, with all possible Dispatch, to visit, and deliver a Letter to the *French* Commandant, of very great Importance to your Brothers, the *English;* and I dare say to you their Friends and allies.

I was desired, Brothers, by your Brother the Governor, to call upon you, the Sachems of the Nation, to inform you of it, and to ask your Advice and Assistance to proceed the nearest and best Road to the *French*. You see, Brothers, I have gotten thus far on my Journey.

His Honour likewise desired me to apply to you for some of your young Men, to conduct and provide Provisions for us on our Way; and be a safe-guard against those *French Indians* who have taken up the hatchet against us. I have spoken this particularly to you Brothers, because his Honor the Governor treats you as good Friends and Allies; and holds you in great Esteem. To confirm what I have said, I give you this string of Wampum.

Washington's mission was ostensibly to the French, but he lost no opportunity on his journey to gain as best he could the friendship of the savages. Washington's interesting journal continues:

We set out about 9 o'Clock with the Half-King Jaskakake, *White Thunder*, and the Hunter; and travelled on the Road to *Venango*, (about one hundred miles from Logstown), where we arrived the 4th of *December*, without any Thing remarkable happening but a continuous Series of bad Weather. . . .

We found the *French* Colours hoisted at a House from which they had driven Mr. *John Frazier*, an *English Subject*. I immediately repaired to it, to know where the Commander resided. There were three Officers, one of whom, Capt. Joncaire, informed me, that he had the command of the Ohio: But that there was a General Officer at the near Fort, where he advised me to apply for an Answer. He invited us to sup with them, and treated us with the greatest Complaisance.

The Wine, as they dosed themselves pretty plentifully with it, soon banished the Restraint which at first appeared in their Conversation; and gave a License to their Tongues to reveal their Sentiments more freely.

They told me, That it was their absolute Design to take Possession of the *Ohio*, and by G— they would do it: For that altho' they were sensible the *English* could raise two Men for their one; yet they knew their Motions were too slow and dilatory to prevent any Undertaking of theirs. They pretend to have an undoubted Right to the River, from a discovery made by one La Salle 60 Years ago; and the Rise of this Expedition is, to prevent our settling on the River or Waters of it, as they had heard of some Families moving-out in Order thereto.

Not without difficulty having gotten his party together again, Washington set out, December 7, for Fort Le Boeuf, some sixty miles to the north. The Journal record continues:

We found it extremely difficult to get the Indians off to-day, as every Stratagem had been used to prevent their going-up with me. . . .

At 11 o'Clock we set out for the Fort, and were prevented from arriving, there till the 11th by excessive Rains, Snows, and bad Travelling, through many Mires and Swamps. . . .

We passed over much good land since we left *Venango*, and through several extensive and very rich Meadows; one of which I believe was near four Miles in Length, and considerably wide in some Places.

Washington found the French commander at Fort Le Bœuf, the Chevalier de St. Pierre, a dignified, courtly gentleman, past middle age, a knight of the military order of St. Louis, and urbane in manner. He extended every courtesy to Washington and his attendants and assured his visitors that he would give his immediate attention to the letter from the Virginia governor. Dinwiddie's message to him had been brief but significant:

The lands upon the River Ohio, in the western parts of the Colony of Virginia, are so notoriously known to be the property of the Crown of Great Britain that it is a matter of equal concern and surprise to me, to hear that a body of French forces are erecting fortresses and making settlements upon that river, within his Majesty's Dominions. The many and repeated complaints that I have received of these acts of hostility lay me under the necessity of sending . . . George Washington, Esq. . . . to complain to you of the encroachments thus made, and of the injuries done to the subjects of Great Britain, in violation of the law of nations, and the treaties now subsisting between the two Crowns.[2]

It was developed on this journey of Washington's that Dinwiddie had selected a rare man as his messenger. Young as he was, Washington had a sharp eye for strategic points in case of hostilities. He especially recommended to Dinwiddie that a fort be placed at the confluence of the Alleghany and Monongahela Rivers, known then as the "Forks of the Ohio." Washington's observations, on this journey, which included the French positions, force, and temper, were noted in his journal which Governor Dinwiddie prized so highly that he had it published in the colonial papers for the benefit of the colonies and sent also to London to be published there.[3]

[2] New York Colonial Documents, vol. x, p. 258 (omitted from the Dinwiddie Papers). Dinwiddie's authority was a letter, dated August 28, 1753, of "Instructions for our trusty & welbeloved Robert Dinwiddie . . . with the Advice our Privy Council" from George II to "repell Force by Force" (Loudoun Papers, A. D. S. copy).
[3] Campbell, p. 463.

237] WASHINGTON IN FRENCH AND INDIAN WAR 53

The report which Washington brought back to Governor
Dinwiddie made clear that the colonies must prepare to resist
French encroachment. What is known in history as the
French and Indian War was evidently at hand, and Virginia's governor, by force of circumstances, was destined to
take a more prominent part in it than any other of the
colonial executives. In a certain sense it was Dinwiddie's
war for it was begun in his attempt to protect Virginia territory. The first hostile forces sent out were Virginians; the
first blood was shed by Virginians. Associated with Dinwiddie was Washington, who from the time he bore the governor's first message to the French commander, became so
identified with the struggle against the French that he was
the sword of this war almost as he was later of the one with
the Mother Country.

Washington's return to Williamsburg and his report to
Governor Dinwiddie occasioned the calling of the third session of the assembly (of 1752-1753) as we have noted. But
before this session was called Dinwiddie had already, in cooperation with the Ohio Company, dispatched Captain William
Trent, January, 1754, with a party of thirty-three men, to
the Forks of the Ohio, to erect a fort at that point. Trent
had formerly visited this section as a scout. Dinwiddie seems
to have commissioned Captain Trent to enlist, in addition to
the thirty-three men above mentioned, one hundred more from
among the traders on the border. To back up the work of
Trent, Dinwiddie prepared to dispatch Washington a second
time to the frontier with two hundred armed men. Washington's second expedition to the frontier was not made,
however, until after the meeting of the third session of the
assembly. Dinwiddie, nevertheless, was acting in the interim
with the advice of his council. He hoped, of course, that
the assembly would not only endorse his action, but provide
ample funds for whatever steps might be necessary fully to
protect Virginia's frontier. His words concerning the dis-
patching of both Captain Trent and Major Washington to
the frontier are given in a letter which he wrote to Lord
Fairfax in January, 1754:

I therefore, with advice of the council, think proper to send immediately out 200 Men to protect those already sent by the Ohio Comp' to build a Fort, and to resist any Attempts on them. I have commission'd Major George Washington, the Bearer hereof, to command 100 men to be rais'd in Frederick County, and Augusta. . . . Capt. Wm. Trent has my Com'd to enlist 100 more men among the Traders &c.[4]

From the Pennsylvania Archives, quoted by Ford in his "Writings of Washington," we have an interesting sidelight on the character of Trent's force, upon the part that Washington played, and incidentally upon Pennsylvania's attitude in the early days of the French and Indian War:

In consequence of a free consent given . . . by the Indians to build store houses on the Ohio, no other force (was) sent than about 30 half-starved ordinary men, under a very improper commander, Capt. Trent; who when building a small ill constructed house at the mouth of the Monongealo, the Govt. of Virginia sent Mr. Washington to summon ye French Commander on the River B. . . ., & on his haughty answer, raised a few forces, expecting ye Province of Pennsylvania wou'd have either sent men, or given a large sum to enlist such as you'd enter Volunteers, but found that instead of affording assistance they fell into disputes with their Gov'r, & seemed to espouse the French claims.[5]

There is some difficulty in disentangling events connected with Washington's second mission to the Virginia Frontier. The facts appear to be as follows: Governor Dinwiddie having already, with the advice of his council, and the cooperation of the Ohio Company, sent Captain William Trent in mid-winter to erect a fort at the Forks of the Ohio where Washington thought one should be erected, proposed to back up the movements of Trent as soon as possible. Washington was ordered to Alexandria, Virginia, where he was to concentrate a force that was being raised in Frederick and Augusta counties. In the meantime, the third session of the Virginia assembly met, but due to circumstances already spoken of, failed to accomplish anything definite. Notwithstanding the disappointment that Dinwiddie felt because of the attitude of the assembly, he decided to increase the force to be sent to the frontier to six small companies of

---

[4] Dinwiddie Papers, vol. i, p. 49.
[5] Pennsylvania Archives, vol. ii, p. 238, quoted by Ford, Writings of Washington, vol. i, p. 40 n.

fifty men each. This entire force he proposed to put under Washington who was to be commissioned colonel. But Washington, thinking he was too young for such a responsible position, declined the offer, and, as a consequence Joshua Fry was commissioned colonel and put in command of all the forces. Washington, on the other hand, was made lieutenant-colonel, and, as matters turned out, bore the brunt of the entire campaign.

After considerable delay in getting together men and supplies, Washington left Alexandria, April 2, 1754, and proceeded to Wills Creek (now Cumberland, Maryland) by way of Winchester. In explanation of the difficulty that Washington had in recruiting men for the expedition, the following letter, under date of March 7, 1754, written to Dinwiddie from Alexandria, speaks for itself:

> Honble. Sir,
> It is now grown a pretty general clamor; . . . some of those, who were among the first enlisters, being needy, . . . are very importunate to receive their due. I have soothed and quieted them as much as possible, under pretense of receiving your Honour's instructions. . . . I have increased my number of men to about 25, . . . I should have several more, if excessive bad weather did not prevent their meeting agreeable to their officers' commands. . . . We find the generality of those who are enlisted, are of those loose, idle persons, that are quite destitute of house and home, and . . . many of them of cloathes. . . . Many of them are without shoes, others want stockings, some are without shirts, and not a few that have scarce a coat or a waistcoat to their backs. . . . But I believe really every man of them, for their own credit's sake, is willing to be cloathed at their own expense. . . .[6]

When Washington arrived at Wills Creek, April 20, 1754, in command of about one hundred and fifty men, he learned of the disaster that had befallen Trent and his men. Five days later Trent's men returning from the Forks of the Ohio reached Wills Creek where Washington was. It seems that Trent had built in part a fort at the point designated at the Forks of the Ohio, and leaving Ensign Ward in charge [7] of the unfinished work, had returned to Wills Creek on private business. In the meantime, a French force of considerable numbers had compelled Ward and his men to

---

[6] Ford, Writings of Washington, vol. i, p. 42.
[7] New York Colonial Documents, vol. vi, p. 840.

leave their unfinished fort and to quit that part of the frontier.

Colonel Fry had not as yet arrived at Wills Creek, and his non-arrival in connection with the miscarriage of Trent's plans, combined to place Washington in a very trying situation. He felt the necessity of reaching the Forks of the Ohio as soon as possible. He called a council of war, wrote some urgent letters to the governors of the colonies asking them to give him any assistance they could, and resolved to push on towards the Forks without waiting for Colonel Fry. It is well in this connection to know what were Washington's instructions in regard to the treatment of the French and their Indian allies. War had not been declared, yet it was imminent. Dinwiddie was inclined to look upon the treatment of Trent and his men as an act of open hostility on the part of the French. In fact, Dinwiddie regarded the occupation of the ground by the French as an act of hostility. Washington's commission says, among other things:

> You are to act on the Defensive, but in Case any Attempts are made to obstruct the Works or interrupt our Settlem'ts by any Persons whatsoever You are to restrain all such Offenders, and in Case of resistance to make Prisoners of or kill and destroy them. . . .[8]

As Washington and his men approached a place called Great Meadows, he learned that a party of French were marching towards him, determined to attack the first English they should meet.[9] The famous encounter [10] with M. de Jumonville was the result. The pros and cons of this incident are too well known to call for detailed mention here. Jumonville and some of his men were killed. Washington by this act practically " crossed the Rubicon."

The killing of Jumonville called forth a counter attack [11] from the French, led by Jumonville's brother, and was the occasion of Washington's building the rude fort known as

---

[8] Dinwiddie Papers, vol. i, p. 59.
[9] Virginia Historical Collections, vol. i, pp. 225-228.
[10] May 28, 1754.
[11] Dinwiddie Papers, vol. i, pp. 239-243.

Fort Necessity.[12] The French far outnumbered Washington's force,[13] but were chary of a near approach to his rude fortification. Both forces were firing at long range, and after some losses on both sides, the French commander suggested such remarkable terms [14] to Washington, not knowing, probably, the weakness of Washington's force, that the colonial commander felt compelled to accept them and marched away with the honors of war. This is known as the capitulation of Fort Necessity and created no little consternation at the capital of the Virginia colony, following as it did in the wake of the Trent disaster. It was obvious now that Dinwiddie was involved too far to recede from the position he had taken. As a consequence, the colonies must prepare for a struggle for mastery against the French and Indian allies. It should be said here that notwithstanding what, upon the face of it, looked like a defeat of Washington, his conduct in this campaign, as well as that of his troops, was highly commended by the governor, the council, and the house of burgesses.[15] It should be noted here, also, that Colonel Fry who got no further than Wills Creek died while Washington was fighting at Great Meadows. Washington thus became commander of the expedition.

This brings us logically to the fourth session of the assembly (of 1752-1755) which began August 22, 1754. It was this session, as we have before noted, that heard the last echo of the famous " pistole fee," which nullified an otherwise generous bill providing twenty thousand pounds for campaign purposes. The rider to this bill with its provision to pay Peyton Randolph £2,500, effectively killed the bill,[16] and thus the session of the assembly did nothing for

---

[12] See Minutes of a Council of War in Washington's handwriting, held at Gist's plantation, June 28, 1754 (Hamilton, vol. i, pp. 16-18).

[13] See Roll of Officers and soldiers, Washington, MSS., vol. i, p. 44.

[14] Pennsylvania Archives, vol. ii, pp. 145-146.

[15] Journals, 1752-1755, p. 198; Hamilton, vol. i, pp. 45-46; Charles Carter to Washington, June 5, 1754, Washington, MSS., vol. i, p. 32.

[16] Dinwiddie Papers, vol. i, p. 324.

the frontier that at this time was in so precarious a condition.

The fifth session of the assembly[17] met closely upon the heels of the adjournment of the fourth. The burgesses by this time had apparently come to themselves, and the pistole fee affair having been settled to the satisfaction of all parties concerned, a bill was promptly passed for raising by poll tax twenty thousand pounds for the protection of the frontier.[18] The assembly also passed a bill compelling all able-bodied men who had no visible means of support to serve as soldiers.[19] At the meeting of this session, Governor Dinwiddie announced [20] that the king had sent ten thousand pounds, besides military stores, for use in the protection of the colony of Virginia.

It was now late in the fall of 1754. Notwithstanding the proximity of winter, Governor Dinwiddie would have had Washington with the forces [21] that were now mustered march across the Alleghanies and drive the French from Fort Duquesne. Washington remonstrated in very strong language against such a suicidal policy, and the proposed campaign was for the time abandoned. But the untiring Dinwiddie spent the winter months in forming new plans [22] and enlarging the little army for a campaign in the coming spring. Dinwiddie's scheme[23] of reorganizing the military forces of the colony, in line with the policy of the home government, was to put the entire colonial forces on the basis of the regular establishment, the highest officers in such an establishment holding the rank of captain.[24] This plan had the effect of reducing Washington to the rank of captain and

---

[17] From October 17-November 2, 1754.

[18] Hening, vol. vi, pp. 435-438.

[19] Ibid., vol. vi, pp. 435-440.

[20] Journals, 1752-1758, p. 209.

[21] H. J. Eckenrode, List of the Colonial Soldiers of Virginia, p. 6.

[22] Dinwiddie to Lord Halifax, Nov. 16, 1754, Dinwiddie Papers, vol. i, pp. 405-406; Dinwiddie to Earl Granville and to James Abercrombie, Nov. 16, 1754, ibid., pp. 407-411.

[23] Ford, Writings of Washington, vol. i, p. 137 n.

[24] A facsimile of the king's order for settling disputes regarding rank and command, November 12, 1754, is given by Hamilton, vol. i, p. 56.

placing him under men whom he had formerly commanded. Indignant at such a procedure, he resigned his commission. Washington passed the winter in retirement awaiting the developments of the spring. Those developments came in the way of a great surprise which at the time sent a thrill of joy through the entire body of colonies. Governor Dinwiddie, at the sixth session of the assembly, May 1, 1755, had the pleasure of announcing that General Braddock had been sent from England with two regiments to " drive the French from the Ohio Valley." [25]

This brings us to a turning point in the French and Indian War. So far the efforts to resist the French had been confined largely, if not entirely, to the Virginia Frontier, and to Dinwiddie as the governor of the colony. It has been seen already that the Virginia governor was sorely tried over the attitude which most of the other colonies had taken towards the claims of the French to the Ohio and Mississippi Valleys and towards the French disposition to limit the English to the Atlantic Coast. As long as Dinwiddie (though sixty-three years old[26] and suffering from the debilitating influence of a stroke of paralysis) was able to meet the emergency; and as long as a young Virginia officer was displaying talents and energy in frontier fighting which later astonished the world,—Virginia's sister colonies were satisfied to let the contest be confined largely to Dinwiddie, Washington, and the inhabitants of Virginia. But when in answer to the persistent calls from Governor Dinwiddie, England at last was aroused to do something worth while, and, having sent a fleet into the Northern Atlantic waters to intercept reinforcements from France, also sent General Braddock to America with two regular regiments, with orders to make Virginia his base—then colonial interest in the contest began to take form all along the Atlantic Coast. From this time on, the French and Indian War lost its practically local char-

---

[25] Journals, 1752-1758, p. 231.

[26] Dinwiddie Papers, vol. i, p. 11; for a typical example of Dinwiddie's continued leadership in colonial defence, see Dinwiddie to the Earl of Loudoun, August 28, 1756, Loudoun Papers, A. D. S.

acter, and became the war of the entire English-speaking contingent in America against the French.

For the reasons just given, it seems necessary for a proper appreciation of the significance of the coming of Braddock to state here the relations which the colonies had with the Indians at that time, either in attempts to gain their friendship or to drive them back before the advance of the white man. It is necessary also to show what inducements had been held out to frontiersmen to settle upon the extreme borders of the colonies, and particularly of the Virginia colony, that protection might thereby be given to the interior. The exact boundaries of the Virginia colony should also be made clear, or at least as clear as practicable without going into tedious controversy. The reader will be helped also to an appreciation of this epoch in American history by knowing who were the executives of the various colonies and what they stood for.

A logical beginning will be the boundaries of the Virginia colony at this time: The claim of Virginia to the west and northwest was based upon the grant of land in her third charter, dated June 2, 1609. This original grant was, however, successfully cut down by the Crown, through the issuance of charters to Maryland, the Carolinas, and Pennsylvania. The immense territory that was hers at the time of the French and Indian War included what is now western Pennsylvania, and the present States of West Virginia, Kentucky, Ohio, Indiana, Illinois, Michigan, and Wisconsin. The words of her charter[27] are plain:

We do also . . . Give, Grant, and Confirm, unto the said Treasurer and Co., and their Successors, under the Reservations, Limitations, and Declarations hereafter expressed, all those Lands, Countries, and Territories, situate, lying, and being, in that Part of America called Virginia, from the Point of Land, called Cape or Point Comfort, all along the Sea Coast, to the Northward 200 Miles, and from the said Point of Cape Comfort, all along the Sea Coast, to the South-ward 200 Miles, and all that Space and Circuit of Land, lying from the Sea Coast of the Precinct aforesaid, up into the

---

[27] William MacDonald, Select Charters of American History, p. 11; western North Carolina was thought for many years to be in Virginia.

Land, throughout from Sea to Sea, West and Northwest; and also all the Islands lying within 100 Miles, along the Coast of both Seas of the Precinct aforesaid. . . .

This grant gave Virginia a good title to the famous Forks of the Ohio, where the city of Pittsburgh now stands. The controversy that Virginia had with Pennsylvania over the western boundary line (and which was not settled until 1779) grew out of the ambiguous wording of the Pennsylvania [28] charter of March 4-14, 1681.[29] This charter extended the grant to the Penns westward five degrees of longitude from the Delaware River, or about two hundred and sixty-seven miles. As we know, the Delaware River makes several bends in its course from north to south. The question, therefore, was the exact point from which the line should be started. If the five degrees of longitude were reckoned from the eastern bend of the Delaware, then Pennsylvania's western limits would fall short of the Forks of the Ohio; while if the starting point were the western bend of the Delaware, the extreme limits of the colony would coincide with the present western boundary of that State. Naturally, Virginia contended that the grant contemplated the eastern bend of the Delaware River as the point of measurement, while Pennsylvania just as stoutly maintained that the other bend was the one originally intended for her to use in computing the boundary line.

In the matter of attitude to the Indians of North America, the British officials were correct in principle, but often short-sighted in practice. Urgent messages were sent from the Home Government to the colonies to make friends with the Indians. This was sane advice, but the Lords of Trade themselves knew little of Indian character. Governor Dinwiddie seems, in his zeal, to have undertaken to play the role of William Penn, but the governor overestimated his

[28] Ibid., p. 183.
[29] The system of double dating occurs between the first of January and the 25th of March, from 1582 to 1752, in English-speaking countries. By an act of Parliament it became mandatory to discard the system after December 31, 1751, and reckon the first of January as the first of the new year 1752, and every succeeding year thereafter.

ability as a peace-maker, and, as a consequence, was later very pessimistic at Indian professions of friendship, particularly after he had himself failed to accomplish results from a proposed conference with them at Winchester, in May, 1754. He anticipated great things from that conference. In his address to the house of burgesses, November 1, 1753, he said:

As I intend to meet the Chiefs of the different Tribes of Indians next May, at Winchester, to deliver a very considerable Present from his Majesty; I am in great Hopes then, to make a firm, strong, and lasting Alliance with them.[30]

When " next May " came, Governor Dinwiddie was on the ground, expecting to meet and conquer. His letters, however, indicate that his great expectations ended in " three strings of wampum "! He said in a letter to Sir Thomas Robinson, June 18, 1754: " I waited in that Town (Winchester) for sixteen days, in expectation of the Indians, agreeable to their promise. I received a Message from some of the Chiefs of their Tribes acquainting me that they could not come to me at that time . . . but desired me to send some of the Present sent them by their Father, the King of Great Britain." [31] Later, in another letter,[32] Dinwiddie said: " My endeavours to obtain the Friendship of the Indians has been constant, and I had the pleasure at Winchester to receive three strings of Wampum from the Wyandotts and other Tribes of Indians." He expressed the hope, however, that the Conference at Albany, of which we shall speak later, would result in the " Six Nations taking up the Hatchet against the French, which will put Spirits into all the other Nations of Indians." But on August 15, of the same year, he said: " Our Colonies met the Chiefs of the Six Nations but they were not able to prevail with them to take up the Hatchet against the French, but pretend to remain Neuter, till they see the success of either the Contending Parties." [33] And then more in detail, Dinwiddie

---

[30] Journals, 1752-1758, p. 104.
[31] Dinwiddie Papers, vol. i, pp. 201-202.
[32] Dinwiddie to the Lords of Trade, June 18, 1754, ibid., vol. i, p. 207.
[33] Dinwiddie to James Abercrombie, ibid., vol. i, p. 285.

wrote his opinion of Indians in a letter to Governor Hamilton, of Pennsylvania, under date, July 31, 1754:

> Mr. Washington had many of the Indians with him, but I observe these People remain inactive till they see how Affairs go, and, generally speaking, side with the Conquerors; yet in my private Opinion, little dependence is to be put in them.[34]

Governor Dinwiddie had started out with optimistic sentiments concerning Indian loyalty and the possibilities of making staunch friends of them; he had swung to the other extreme of almost complete loss of faith in their professions of friendship. In this connection it may be well to give extracts of a letter from Washington to Governor Dinwiddie, indicating how a practiced hand dealt with the Indians, having back of that hand a proper conception of Indian character. Washington, under date of May 18, 1754, said:

> As I shall have frequent communications with the Indians, *which is of no effect without Wampum*, I hope your Honour will order some to be sent—indeed we ought to have Spirit, and many other things of this sort, which is always expected by every Indian that brings a Message of good report; also the Chiefs who visit and converse in Council look for it. . . . I would recommend some of the Treaty Goods being sent for that purpose; . . . this is the method the French pursue, and a trifle judiciously bestowed, and in season, may turn to our advantage.[35]

On June 19, 1754, the celebrated Albany Congress met. This was called at the instance of the Home Government which had sent out circular letters to the governors of the colonies, asking them to send representatives to this meeting. The purpose of the conference was to cement an alliance with the Indians, known as the Six Nations, and to evolve some plan of concerted action against the French on the part of the colonies. The Six Nations, more generally called the Iroquois, dwelt in western New York and had always been strongly pro-English.[36] Their presence provided a buffer community between the northern English colonies and the encroaching French. But as war became imminent

---

[34] Ibid., vol. i, p. 256.

[35] Ibid., vol. i, p. 170. Dinwiddie, writing to Washington, June 27, 1754, said: "I have order'd two Hhds. of rum out" (ibid., p. 222). Brock states that "The cost of rum at this period was 3s. 6d. a gallon."

[36] See Appendix II, p. 150.

between the English and French, the latter were very active in an endeavor to alienate the Six Nations from the English. The Albany conference succeeded in at least keeping the Six Nations neutral, though the conference would have preferred, as Dinwiddie said, "that they take up the hatchet against the French." The second feature of the conference was a failure, notwithstanding the fact that Benjamin Franklin proposed a scheme of union. The reason given why Virginia did not send a representative to this conference was because the Virginia assembly, Dinwiddie said, "c'd not be prevailed on to appoint Com's [commissioners]." Governor Dinwiddie, however, wrote to Governor De Lancey to appear in behalf of Virginia.[37] All of the English colonies were represented except New Jersey, Virginia, and the Carolinas. At a critical point in the Albany conference, the English would have lost their grip upon the wavering Iroquois but for the influence of William Johnson, a hardy Irish frontiersman who understood Indian character, and kept them true to the English. Washington also seems to have been one of those men whom the Indians both loved and feared and who appears never to have lost his influence over Indians who had once become attached to him.

While the colonists endeavored first of all to make peace with the Indians and if possible to win their support in the French and Indian War, a second course was pursued where the Indians were hopelessly antagonistic. This was the uncanny plan of offering £10 and even more for the scalp of an enemy Indian who was a male and over twelve years of

---

[37] Dinwiddie Papers, vol. i, p. 364. On the Albany Congress, see New York Colonial Documents, vol. vi, pp. 853-897. The Six Nations were called Iroquois by the French, Maqua by the Dutch, Mingoes by the English, and Mengwee by the other Indian nations. Their home was in New York, but they were a warlike people and their conquests extended from New York to Carolina, and from New England to the Mississippi. Their warriors were estimated in 1660 by the French to be 2,200; Bancroft assumed their "just numbers," including their allies and southern kindred, as about 17,000 (R. A. Brock, Dinwiddie Papers, vol. i, pp. 12, 19, from Olden Time, vol. i, pp. 4, 386-396).

age. This custom[38] first became a law in New England and afterwards in Virginia. While this practice was much abused, it had much to do with the annihilation of those Indians whom it was impossible to win over to friendship with the English. The Indians who were friendly joined the English with great alacrity in this scalping project for the sake of the reward.

Early in the year 1754, the resourceful mind of Governor Dinwiddie had developed a plan both to encourage immigration to the Ohio valley and also to protect the extreme frontier of Virginia. He issued a proclamation [39] allotting 200,000 acres of land along the Ohio River, to be distributed among the men who would serve in the French and Indian War and who would settle in that section of the country. This land was to be free from taxes for a period of fifteen years, and the settlers were to have fort protection. Had Washington's expedition, which ended in his capitulation, succeeded, as Dinwiddie felt sure it would, the tract of land on the Ohio doubtless would have been taken up by eager frontiersmen. But the defeat of Trent, then of Washington, and later of Braddock, rendered this laudable scheme of Dinwiddie's impracticable.

No summary of the general situation at the time of Braddock's expedition would be complete without a brief reference to the attitude of the different colonies to a war which up to this time had been very largely one between the Virginia colony and the French and Indians on her borders. Massachusetts may be taken as typical of New England, and

---

[38] Journals, 1752-55, p. 298; Hening, vol. vi, pp. 551, 552, 565, vol. vii, pp. 121-123; Ford, Writings of Washington, vol. i, p. 238.

[39] Dinwiddie to Lord Holdernesse, March 12, 1754, Dinwiddie Papers, vol. i, p. 96; Hening, vol. vii, pp. 661-662; Draper, MSS., 3ZZ46 (Virginia Papers), has a contemporary copy dated February 19, 1754. King George II in a letter to Dinwiddie dated August 28, 1753, mentions having received a letter from him even as early as June 16, 1753. regarding the problems of frontier defense and the "utility of building Some Forts upon the River Ohio in the Western Part of our Colony of Virginia, for the Security and Protection of our Subjects, & of the Indians in Alliance with us. . . ." (Loudoun Papers, Dinwiddie file, 1753, A. D. S. copy; omitted from published Dinwiddie Papers).

Governor William Shirley[40] of that colony exhibited the readiness of New England to do her part in the struggle. There is little doubt that of all the governors of the colonies at the time of which we write, Dinwiddie of Virginia and Shirley of Massachusetts were the strongest. New England had been prominent in wars with the Indians previous to this, and with the " papist " French to the north and west of her, and she had her sword well whetted for a conflict with these border foes. New York was one of the colonies which had taken the position that it was not clear whether the French had really encroached upon Virginia territory by erecting forts at Presqu' Isle and Le Boeuf and also at Venango, where they drove off a body of English who had established a trading post. Whether this position taken by New York was a sincere one, or simply an excuse given for indifference concerning what disposition was made of the Ohio and Mississippi valleys, is not clear. We know that two independent companies sent from New York to the aid of Dinwiddie in the Washington expedition to Great Meadows, arrived too late to be of any service and Dinwiddie candidly told the governor of New York that this tardiness occasioned the defeat of Washington there. Pennsylvania was dominated largely by Quakers and embarrassed, as we have seen, by its proprietary character and, added to all this, contained a large population of unassimilated Germans. The relations between Governor Dinwiddie and Governor Hamilton seem to have been cordial, but the Pennsylvania colony up to the coming of Braddock, had played a sorry part in assisting in the defense of the frontier. The New Jersey [41] colony under Governor Belcher seems to have had small sympathy with Governor Dinwiddie's zeal to defend the western frontier and to extend English domains to the utmost limit. Maryland had an excellent governor in Sharpe,

---

[40] Governor, 1740-1756.

[41] See Dinwiddie to Belcher, November 8, 1754, Dinwiddie Papers, vol. i, p. 392; Dinwiddie to Belcher, January 14, 1755, ibid., vol. i, pp. 457-458; Dinwiddie to Lords of Trade, ibid., vol. i, p. 279; see Appendix II, No. 8; see below, pp. 171-172.

who did all that he could with a proprietary [42] colony that
was at variance with the proprietor, and, as has been seen
already, was disinclined to vote anything for the protection
of the frontier unless their proprietor would agree to having
his own land taxed.   Maryland, however, did come to Dinwiddie's aid in helping to garrison Fort Cumberland and in
voting six thousand pounds for defense.   What Maryland
lacked in cooperation with Dinwiddie, its governor, Sharpe,[43]
largely atoned for in his cordial feelings towards the Virginia governor, with whom he was in constant correspondence.   North Carolina was perhaps the colony in the south
that responded most cordially and promptly to the governor
of Virginia in his attempt to defend the frontier.   Governor
Dobbs was one of the strongest of the colonial governors at
this time.   His colony was represented at Great Meadows
by two independent companies.[44]   Governor Glen of South
Carolina assumed an antagonistic attitude [45] toward Governor
Dinwiddie, and the relations between the two men were
somewhat strained.   A South Carolina company of inde-
pendents was at Great Meadows, but their commander, Mc-
Kay, annoyed Washington not a little by refusing to take
orders from him.   At the same time, Virginia and South
Carolina in point of nationality, creed, and in the spirit of
the people, were most alike of all the colonies south of New
England.

This brief review indicates that there was little cohesion,
little cooperation, and no centralized power, among the colonies at the time when General Braddock landed at Hamp-

---

[42] J. W. Black, " Maryland's Attitude in the Struggle for Canada "
in the Johns Hopkins University Studies, series X, pp. 315-365;
Dinwiddie to Earl of Halifax, May 24, 1756, Dinwiddie Papers,
vol. ii, pp. 417-418; see Appendix II, No. 8.

[43] For a short time in command of the forces of the southern
colonies.   See letter from Annapolis, March 8, 1756, " To the Commanding Officer of the Virginia Forces " (Hamilton, vol. i, pp.
201-202).

[44] Hamilton, vol. i, pp. 20-23.   Arthur Dobbs was Governor of North
Carolina from November 1, 1754, until his death, March 28, 1765.

[45] Dinwiddie to Lords of Trade, October 25, 1754, Dinwiddie Papers,
vol. i, p. 362; Dinwiddie to Glen, August 5, 1754, ibid., vol. i, pp.
272-276.

ton Roads. The coming of General Braddock concentrated interest upon the struggle that up until then had been limited to the Virginia Frontier; the defeat of General Braddock aroused most of the colonies, at least to self-protection, so that there was union of effort after that disaster which it did not seem possible to have before.

Returning now to Braddock's arrival in America, its influence was at once apparent in a conference of colonial governors at Alexandria, Virginia.[46] Early in March, 1755, the general proceeded to the capital of the Virginia colony, Williamsburg, and sent out a call for the governors of the various colonies to meet him at Alexandria.[47] On April 14, he conferred with governors Shirley of Massachusetts, Dinwiddie of Virginia, De Lancey of New York, Sharpe of Maryland, Morris of Pennsylvania, and Dobbs of North Carolina. The result of this council of war, as it turned out to be, was as follows: Braddock was to advance against Fort Duquesne; Governor Shirley, next in command to Braddock, was to lead a force against Niagara and Frontenac; and William Johnson, the expert Indian master, was to move against Crown Point, on Lake Champlain. The time fixed for concerted action was the end of June—only about two months off.

Interest naturally gathers about General Braddock and his famous 44th and 48th regiments of English regulars. The story of his expedition is known to every schoolboy of America. In reading the records [48] of this romantic but disastrous campaign, admiration for the unfortunate Braddock's bravery almost eclipses our disgust at his autocracy, and his insensibility to conditions he must meet in a campaign more like one in the jungles of Africa than like the

[46] Ford, Writings of Washington, vol. i, p. 151n.; references to Documentary History of New York, vol. ii, p. 376.

[47] Annapolis was at first named as the place of meeting.

[48] Wisconsin Historical Collections, vol. iii, pp. 212-215; vol. vii, pp. 130-135; Francis Parkman, Montcalm and Wolfe, vol. ii, pp. 425-426. The Loudoun Papers contain contemporary copies of Braddock's letters, 1755, and typical of their general fault-finding tenor is a letter from Braddock to Sir Thomas Robinson written from Fort Cumberland, June 5, 1755.

chariot-borne, band-playing, elegantly-uniformed expedition he had provided for. Braddock was not a young officer, but a seasoned British commander of proven ability and daring. His hobby was discipline, although he seems to have exempted himself from restraints he would impose on others. If bursts of temper, oaths of monstrous sort, hard drinking, and intemperate eating come within the purview of soldierly discipline, then Braddock was an undisciplined man. His confidence in his ability to make short work of both French and Indians reminds us at once of Pitcairn at Concord. His petulance at the delay of recruits and provisions found vent in execrations on everything connected with the American colonies. He at least saw the worth of two Americans, even if he did not always accept their advice. He at once called George Washington out of retirement,[49] and made him one of his aides. He also saw in Benjamin Franklin " almost the only Instance of ability and honesty " he had found in all the colonies.[50] Franklin's shrewdness served Braddock well, but the general never knew, probably, how the dress of Sir John St. Clair, who was with Braddock and was in the uniform of a Hussar, (as Franklin took it to be), gave Franklin the key with which he unlocked the treasures of the Dutch farmers of Pennsylvania and thus procured for Braddock all the wagons and pack horses he needed. Franklin, knowing how the Germans in their old country had dreaded the Hussars, wrote a circular letter to the Dutch of Lancaster, York and Cumberland counties, telling them that " he supposed that Sir John St. Clair, the Hussar, with a

[49] Washington resigned his commission in October, 1754, because, under Governor Dinwiddie's newly-devised military establishment of ten independent companies, of 100 men each, there was no rank above that of captain, and commissions held from Dinwiddie were subordinate to those from the King. The effect was to reduce Colonel Washington to the rank of captain, and to place him under officers whom he had commanded. He remained in private life, at Mount Vernon, until the arrival of Braddock, who called him to his staff by letter dated March 2, 1755 (R. A. Brock in Dinwiddie Papers, vol. i, p. 403n.).

[50] Braddock to Sir Thomas Robinson, from Cumberland, June 5, 1755, contemporary copy in Loudoun Papers, Braddock file, 1755.

body of Soldiers" would enter their counties at once and take possession of what wagons and horses they needed— unless those things were given at once. The effect was electrical. The wagons and horses reported promptly at Wills Creek (Cumberland) by the close of June.[51]

It is a temptation to tell in detail of Braddock's march through Fredericktown, Maryland, and thence by Winchester to Cumberland; how he was here introduced to Indians for the first time and looked upon them as he saw their paint, war dances, and heard their yells that startled the night hours, as so many demons let loose from the infernal regions; how his soldiers took advantage of the abandonment of the Indian maidens, led by the princess Bright Lightning, when the Indian girls threw themselves into the arms of the red-coated British whose glorious dress completely captivated them; how Braddock offended such masters of Indian fighting as "Jack, the Black Hunter" by his insistence upon discipline, and thus lost to himself men, any one of whom in an Indian war was equal to a whole company of British regulars; how Braddock's march through the forest to the back country was like a triumphal procession and drew from Washington the remark that he had never seen a more beautiful sight; how, as they drew near to the place of Washington's previous experiences with the French and Indians, Braddock's forces were suddenly attacked by what seemed to be an "invisible foe"; how confusion reached such limits that the only soldiers who were doing effective service in killing the Indians were shot down by Braddock's own men, mistaking them for Frenchmen; how the general and Washington, both alike having horse after horse killed under them, seemed impervious to fear; how the general finally fell, and when his own men left him to welter in his blood, two Virginians whom he had despised for their want of training as soldiers, took up his body at the risk of their lives and carried it to safety; how Braddock [52] in his humiliation, re-

---

[51] W. H. Lowdermilk, History of Cumberland (Maryland), pp. 112-114. 135; Draper, MSS., 1QQ84.

[52] For a letter in vindication of Braddock's conduct, see Captain

gardless of his wounds, thought only of a disaster which he could not understand; how his faithful aide, Washington, whom he would not heed in methods of fighting, read the last rites of the Church over Braddock's body which was buried in the middle of the roadway; how Washington, in a masterly way, though weak from a late serious illness, covered the retreat, and rescued the remnant of the little army from the jaws of death.   Surely, no more pitiable tale of the butchery of brave men, or of disaster following high hopes and great preparations was ever told.   The loss of the battle, with everything which that loss involved, would seem to have been enough to discourage the stoutest hearts from attempting to do more towards conquering the frontier.   Was fate against the British and their claims?

The burgesses of Virginia must have been pricked in conscience at the sight of their governor, already shocked by paralysis, bravely standing up under the blow of Braddock's defeat, when they knew how his hopes had been built on the success of that expedition.   More than any other governor, he felt the force of the disaster, for more than any other governor he had been instrumental in calling the British regulars to the aid of the colonies.   His letters at the time to different governors [53] and to others [54] show how hard it was for him to believe what Colonel Innes, his friend, was the first to write him.   He says: " I never doubted of the General's (Braddock's) success when I considered his forces and the train of his artillery." [55]   He hopes against hope that Colonel Innes' letter that " was wrote in a great hurry,"

Robert Orme to Washington, August 25, 1755 (Hamilton, vol. i, pp. 83-84).   For a remarkable, though depreciative, statement as to Braddock's fitness for leadership in this campaign, see a letter from William Shirley, aid-de-camp and military secretary to General Braddock, and son of General Shirley, to the Hon. Robert Hunter Morris, Lieutenant Governor of Pennsylvania, dated at Fort Cumberland, May 23, 1755 (ibid., pp. 63-66).

[53] Dinwiddie Papers, July 28-29, 1755, vol. ii, pp. 123-129.

[54] Dinwiddie to Colonel James Patton, vol. ii, pp. 92-93, ibid.; Dinwiddie to Captain Robert Orme, pp. 148-149.   For his letters to the officials in England, see ibid., pp. 99, 112, 113, 115, 116, 117, 139, 141.

[55] Ibid., p. 98.

had exaggerated the defeat. But even before he heard the full account from Washington's pen [56] he was planning for a counter attack upon the French ere they could recover from their surprise. Addressing Washington by the very unusual term, " Dear Washington," [57] Dinwiddie wanted to know " Whether with the number of men remaining there is possibility of doing something the other side of the mountain before the winter months." To Colonel Dunbar he deplored that three hundred French and Indians defeated 1,300 British, and adds: " Dear Colonel, is there no method left to retrieve the dishonor done to British arms? " [58] Governor Dinwiddie then appealed to the house of burgesses in a strain that must have impressed them with his sincerity, indomitable courage and resolution.[59] He put his hand at once on the spot that was vital, namely, the open way from Fort Cumberland to the Ohio, by which the enemy could and would pour in upon Virginia and Maryland. He begged the burgesses in the name of the " Virginia forces that purchased immortal glory on the banks of the Monongahela " to preserve " the most invaluable of all human treasures— religious and civil liberty."

The matter to which Governor Dinwiddie alluded—the open way to the interior of Virginia and Maryland—was only one phase of the dismal truth which the colonies had now to face. It was true that the very roadways which had been cut through the forests to reach the foe were now the ways which the foe was using to reach the hearts of the colonies. The situation was almost as though the dykes of Holland had been cut and the ocean had begun its inundation. Through every gap and mountain pass which had hitherto been used by frontiersmen to push toward the west, the gleeful, triumphant savages now rushed in—bold in their confidence that the spirit of the English colonists was broken. The people of the frontier, in panic, rolled back in waves

---

[56] Washington to Dinwiddie, July 18, 1755 (Ford, Writings of Washington, vol. i, p. 175).

[57] Dinwiddie Papers, vol. ii, p. 122.

[58] Ibid., p. 118.

[59] Ibid., pp. 134, 135.

over the mountains into the Shenandoah Valley,—the savages upon their heels, particularly in Augusta county, and even as far down the Valley as Winchester.[60] For a time it looked as if the British would be swept from the American continent.[61]

The burgesses of Virginia had now forgotten their difficulties with their governor and promptly voted [62] £40,000, with which Dinwiddie proposed to augment the Virginia forces so as to have at least 2,000 men for the protection of the colony. The spirit of the Virginians was evidently aroused. The governor says in a letter to Colonel Innes (August 11, 1755), several days after the burgesses had voted to provide the money named above: " I believe they would have given £100,000 if there was any probability of making a second attempt." [63] Evidently, the example of the governor in standing by his guns was having its effect on the Virginia burgesses.

While the governor of Virginia and the people of the colony were preparing in earnest to defend [64] themselves, if

[60] Dinwiddie gives some interesting figures in a letter to Sir Thomas Robinson, July 23, 1755: " After the Gen'l left Fort Cumb'l'd I order'd the Militia to be rais'd in Frederick and Hampshire to defend the Frontier. Some Time after a Numb'r of Fr. and Ind's, 150 in Numb'r, came on our frontiers, committed many robberies and Murders. I found the Militia were a cowardly People or seiz'd with such Pannick as not to resist the Insults of the Enemy. I therefore immediately rais'd three Compa's of Rangers and order'd them to range along our Frontiers to annoy the Enemy and shew them as little Mercy as they have done our poor People. They have murdered about 35. I have order'd the whole Militia of y's Dom'n to be muster'd, their Numb'rs, &c., to be ret'd to me, and . . . I will make a large Draught from each Co'ty . . . to repell Force by Force " (Dinwiddie Papers, vol. ii. pp. 112-113).

[61] Journals, 1752-1755, pp. xxiii, 297-315; Dinwiddie Papers, vol. ii, pp. 96-145.

[62] Ibid., p. 146.

[63] Ibid., p. 146.

[64] Dinwiddie to Colonel James Patton, County-Lieutenant of Augusta County, August 1, 1755, Draper, MSS., 1QQ85, Dinwiddie Papers, vol. ii, pp. 132-133; Dinwiddie to Colonel John Buchanan, of Augusta, August 14, 1755, Draper, MSS., 1QQ86, Dinwiddie Papers, vol. ii, p. 132; David Robinson (from Fort on Catawba) to William Preston, November 14, 1755, Draper, MSS., 1QQ82; Dinwiddie to Preston, April 24, 1756, Draper, MSS., 1QQ125; Colonel Edmund Pendleton to Preston, May 12, 1756, Draper, MSS., 1QQ126-

not to retrieve their losses, it is interesting to know what old Half-King, the head of the Six Nations, thought of the English and of their French foes. Retiring in disgust from any further participation in struggles, such as Braddock's, where a handful of French and Indians defeated over 1,000 English, the old warrior said that while the French were "cowards, the British were fools." It might have been interesting to old Half-King to know how fully Washington agreed with him!

Even before the defeat of Braddock, the Indians had taken advantage of the general concentration of interest and forces upon that expedition and had been guilty of barbarous outrages upon the frontier of Augusta County. It might be well to say here that Hampshire,[65] Frederick and Augusta [66] counties constituted the western frontier of the Virginia colony. Of these counties, Augusta was not only practically unlimited in its depth westward, but in length it took in the greater part of what is now the Shenandoah Valley, and extended to the extreme of Virginia's southern border. Reference to the topography of the region will indicate where the inrush of savages would naturally occur. The gap in the mountains west of Staunton and the one where the James cuts its way through were the danger points, and it was at these points that the Indians most frequently attacked. When the news of Braddock's defeat had been circulated and the import of it understood by the Indian allies of the French, the Virginia Frontier experienced as never before

---

128; Proceedings of a council of war at Augusta Court House, May 20, 1756, Draper, MSS., 1QQ130; Andrew Lewis to Governor Dinwiddie, June, 1756, Draper, MSS., 1QQ131-133. The county-lieutenant (one of the most notable of whom was Colonel James Patton, mentioned above, who met his death at the hands of the Indians late in 1755) was commander-in-chief of the county. This officer, commonly styled "Colonel," was usually a large landed proprietor. He governed the county, and upon him rested the responsibility of a faithful execution of the laws. He could call out the militia when demanded, and account to the governor and counsel for his conduct. The officers of the militia were subject to his orders, and he could organize courts martial (R. A. Brock, Dinwiddie Papers, vol. ii, p. 95n.); see Appendix II, No. 6.

[65] Hening, vol. vi, pp. 376-379.

[66] Ibid., vol. v, pp. 78-79.

pillage and murder. What might have been wantonly done before by Indians following their instincts for plundering and scalping, was now brutally augmented by the thought that the English were their enemies with whom they were at war.

The letters of Dinwiddie and of Washington from the middle of the summer of 1755 to the fall of the following year are burdened with accounts of Indian raids and the panic of the people of Hampshire, Frederick, and Augusta [67] counties. Washington, as late as May, 1756, told Governor Dinwiddie that the roads over the Alleghanies are as much beaten by the French and Indians as they were by Braddock the year before.[68] On April 22, 1756, Washington wrote one of the most remarkable letters [69] to Dinwiddie concerning the distress of the people that was ever penned by him or any other American:

I am too little acquainted, Sir, with pathetic language, to attempt a description of the people's distresses, though I have a generous soul, sensible of wrongs, and swelling for redress. But what can I do? If bleeding, dying! would glut their insatiate revenge, I would be a willing offering to savage fury, and die by inches to save a people! I see their situation, know their danger, and participate their sufferings, without having it in my power to give them further relief, than uncertain promises. In short, I see inevitable destruction in so clear a light, that, unless vigorous measures are taken by the Assembly, and speedy assistance sent from below, the poor inhabitants that are now in forts, must unavoidably fall, while the remainder of the country are flying before the barbarous foe. . . . The supplicating tears of the women, and moving petitions from the men, melt me into such deadly sorrow, that I solemnly declare, if I know my own mind, I could offer myself a willing sacrifice to the butchering enemy, provided that would contribute to the people's ease.

Landon Carter, a burgess from Richmond County, replied to this letter of Washington's in rather unusual language. It shows that he was in full sympathy with Washington and deplored the indifference of the assembly:

---

[67] An interesting autograph document found among the papers of Captain William Preston is a list of his company of rangers, giving the date of enlistment, nationality, age, size, trade, and date of discharge or desertion, from July 16, 1755, to January 1, 1756 (Draper, MSS., 1QQ92).

[68] Ford, Writings of Washington, vol. i, p. 277.

[69] Ibid., vol. i, pp. 248-251.

I think as you do. I have endeavored, though not in the field, yet in the senate, as much as possible to convince the country of danger, and she knows it; but such is her parsimony, that she is willing to wait for the rains to wet the powder, and rats to eat the bowstrings of the enemy, rather than to attempt to drive them from her frontiers.[70]

Washington was made commander-in-chief of the forces of Virginia in August, 1755, and from that date until late in the year of 1757, he was charged with the defense of the frontier. The letters which passed between him and Dinwiddie during this period contain paragraphs that have been interpreted to mean that there was an estrangement between them. No letters, so far as we know, were ever written by Dinwiddie to any third party criticising Washington adversely. He did write letters stating in most respectful terms the few things—usually concerning the occupation and manning of Fort Cumberland—with which he did not agree with Washington. On the other hand, Washington wrote quite freely to his friends concerning the " ambiguous and uncertain way " Governor Dinwiddie gave him instructions. One example of the kind was that written to John Robinson, Speaker of the House of Burgesses, in which the following significant sentences occur in reference to Dinwiddie's commands to him:

My orders are dark, doubtful, and uncertain; today approved, tomorrow condemned. Left to act and proceed at hazard, accountable for consequences, and blamed without the benefit of defense, if you can think my situation capable to excite the smallest degree of envy, or afford the least satisfaction, the truth is hid from you. . . . I am in hope of better regulation on the arrival of Lord Loudoun, to whom I look for the future fate of Virginia. His Lordship, I think, has received impressions tending to prejudice, by false representations of facts, if I may judge from a paragraph of one of his letters to the Governor, on which is founded the resolve to support Fort Cumberland at all events.[71]

---

[70] Ibid., vol. i, p. 251n.

[71] Ibid., vol. i, p. 404. An interesting commentary on the situation is found in the Minutes of a Council of War held at Fort Cumberland, April 16, 1757, given in full in Appendix II, No. 3. John Robinson, from King and Queen County, was elected speaker of the house during the second session of the assembly of 1736-1740 to fill out the unexpired term of Sir John Randolph, who died in 1737. Robinson was held in high esteem and was reelected speaker continuously, and usually unanimously, until 1761.

Speaker Robinson fans the suspicions of Washington by insinuation. In a reply to the above letter, Robinson first blames the Council for action regarding Fort Cumberland which " Was taken before I (Robinson) knew or mistrusted anything." Then follow the words:

Notwithstanding all I could say, they (the Council) persisted in their resolution, without alleging any reason, than that it was in pursuance of Lord Loudoun's desire. It can not be a difficult matter to guess who was the author and promoter of this advice and resolution, or by whom Lord Loudoun has been persuaded, that the place is of such importance.[72]

Out of a situation like this arose a story in the earlier days of our Republic, (and that story has been handed down to other generations), to the effect that Dinwiddie appointed Washington commander-in-chief of the Virginia forces, not because he wished to do it, but because the pressure of public opinion compelled him to do it.[73] As a consequence, Governor Dinwiddie, it is said, was mean enough to annoy Washington and, even as far as he could without being open about it, to frustrate the plans of the man whom he had appointed commander-in-chief of the forces of his colony. With the voluminous correspondence of Dinwiddie before us, it is difficult to conceive how such an idea could have gained credence at all, much less have persisted down to our own times.

Dinwiddie and Washington were alike subjects of Great Britain, alike professing loyalty to that country. The governor was now about sixty-five years old, his handwriting showing the palsied muscles of a paralytic. He was admonished by a second stroke, in October, 1757, that he must no

---

[72] Ibid., vol. i, pp. 406-407.
[73] " Public opinion had subdued the governor's partiality for another candidate, and he acquiesced with apparent satisfaction " (Sparks, vol. i, p. 71). A most remarkable letter, comprehensive to a fault and friendly in its spirit, written by Dinwiddie to Washington, August 19, 1756, is given in full in the Appendix II, No. 4; among the striking examples there given of the governor's confidence in Washington are: " Please write to [certain officials], as I am so much hurried that I have not had time; you may write in my Name;" again, " I think I have fully answer'd Y'r L're, and in what I may be difficient Y'r own Prudence must supply."

longer try to discharge the duties of the office of chief executive of the colony. His letter of October 28, to Lord Loudoun, says: " I've lately been seized with Paralytick Disorder in my head that makes me incapable of discharging the Requisites of my Appointm't in so regular and so exact a Manner as I c'd wish." [74]

Washington, on the other hand, was not twenty-five years old when he was commissioned commander-in-chief of the forces of the colony. He was indebted to Governor Dinwiddie for every military preferment he had so far received. From the time the governor sent him as a mere stripling to the Ohio frontier to bear a message to the French commandant, Dinwiddie had set up the ladder for Washington to climb to usefulness and to fame. If Washington was not made full colonel on the expedition which resulted in the capitulation of Fort Necessity, it was not because Governor Dinwiddie did not offer him that honor. As things turned out, the death of Colonel Fry gave Washington what Dinwiddie would have given him at the beginning. But it is noteworthy, that when the expedition resulted in what was practically a defeat, the generous Dinwiddie was as warm in his congratulations of Washington for his soldiership as though he had subdued the French.

The suggestion that the governor gave the commission of commander-in-chief to Washington against Dinwiddie's own wish and judgment, has about as much basis as the now-exploded idea that the governor was corrupt in handling finances and served as executive of Virginia only for what he could get out of it. The letter that is quoted as indicating that Governor Dinwiddie had a favorite whom he would have made commander-in-chief had he dared, is from Mr. Ludwell, a friend of Washington's, then in the Virginia assembly. That letter is dated August 8, 1755, and says:

[74] Dinwiddie to the Earl of Loudoun, October 28, 1756, Dinwiddie Papers, vol. ii, p. 535; Dinwiddie to the Earl of Loudoun, September 23, 1757, when about to leave Virginia for England, Loudoun Papers, Dinwiddie file.

The House has voted twelve hundred men, but it very probably they will determine at least for four thousand. In conversation with the Governor I said, if this should be done, I supposed his Honor would give the command of them to Colonel Washington, for I thought he deserved everything his country could do for him. The Governor made reply much in your favor, though I understand there is another warm solicitation for it.[75]

On this flimsy foundation is built the theory that Colonel Innes, a countryman of Governor Dinwiddie's, was the favorite with the executive. After Washington's appointment was made, some differences of opinion arose between him and Dinwiddie concerning the occupation of Fort Cumberland, giving occasion for the exchange of some very plain letters between them—hence the further theory that Governor Dinwiddie was never in sympathy with Washington but tried to harass him. Not only did Governor Dinwiddie state frankly to Sir Thomas Robinson, Secretary of State, September 6, 1755, that he had given a commission to " Colonel George Washington, who was one of General Braddock's aid-de-camp," but adds further: " I think (he is) a man of great merit and resolution. . . . I am convinced if General Braddock had survived, he would have recommended Mr. Washington to the royal favor." [76] Before Washington would consent to accept the honor thus conferred on him, he made some stringent demands which Governor Dinwiddie acceded to, which fact furthermore shows how anxious the latter was to have Washington serve in the capacity in which he had been appointed.

Among the outstanding acts of Governor Dinwiddie that have been seized to sustain the position that he was unfriendly to Washington after he had commissioned him commander-in-chief, and that he embarrassed Washington by vague and contradictory commands, at times evincing impatience, are the following. The location and the retention of Fort Cumberland became a bone of contention between Governor Dinwiddie and Colonel Washington. As the fort was located in Maryland, Washington did not feel

---

[75] Ford, Writings of Washington, vol. i, p. 181n.
[76] Dinwiddie Papers, vol. ii, p. 191.

the same responsibility for it that he felt for forts on Virginia soil. He furthermore did not think that a fortification that required so many men to make it effective was wisely placed so far out on the border. To man it, so Washington asserted, would take men from the smaller stockades in the mountain passes and in sparsely settled sections which relied upon them for defense.

It is true that the tenor of the governor's letters sustain the opinion that he preferred retaining and manning Fort Cumberland. An honest review of the pros and cons as to which was the wiser course to pursue, leaves the reader quite uncertain what to think. There was plenty of room for a sincere difference of opinion. But Governor Dinwiddie went so far, after hearing Washington's arguments, as to say:

You know how disagreeable it was to me to give up any Place of Strength, as it w'd raise the Spirits of the Enemy, and at the same time suspect us to be in fear of 'em; and therefore if that Place could be sustained with Safety till Lord Loudoun gives Orders therein, I should be glad; but as you are on the Spot, and You think it very prejudicial to keep the Fortress, I desire You may call a Council of Officers and consult whether most advisable to keep it or demolish it.[77]

Dinwiddie then wrote to Lord Loudoun [78] at length without in any sense injecting his own desires about the fort, save to say that he had hitherto felt that disbanding it would embolden the enemy to make stronger attempts upon the entire frontier. Lord Loudoun replied in words that were quoted to Washington by Dinwiddie as follows: [79] "I do hope and trust that the Government of Virginia will not suffer the Post of F't Cumberland to be wrested from them." Yet in the face of this strong statement, Dinwiddie says to Washington: "Notwithstanding my former Orders, if You and the other Gentlemen Officers think it can be maintained with safety, I shall be glad; which must still be left to your Consultations." The council of war left the matter of Fort Cumberland much as they found it. Governor Dinwiddie

---

[77] September 30, 1756 (Dinwiddie Papers, vol. ii, p. 523).
[78] October 6, 1756 (ibid., vol. ii, p. 525).
[79] October 26, 1756 (ibid., vol. ii, p. 529).

received the report, upon the back of which Washington had given his own opinion, and laid the entire matter before the Council at Williamsburg. That body decided that Fort Cumberland should be maintained and properly manned. Governor Dinwiddie concurred in this opinion. As a consequence, Washington was ordered to " march one hundred men to Fort Cumberland from the forces that were at Winchester."

Previous to this time, when Washington had suggested that Fort Cumberland be abandoned, Governor Dinwiddie had said: " It is a King's Fort and a Magazine for Stores, it's not in my Power to order it be deserted . . . when Lord Loudoun comes here . . . he has full Power to do what he thinks proper, and a Representation to him will be regular."

In a letter [80] written by Washington to John Robinson, August 5, 1756, this letter of Governor Dinwiddie's appears in the following misleading form: " Fort Cumberland is a King's fort, and built chiefly at the charge of the colony, therefore properly under our direction until a governor is appointed." Did some one tamper with Washington's letter, or did the writer, from misrepresentations he had of Governor Dinwiddie's real attitude to both himself and Lord Loudoun, suppose that this was the fair sense of the governor's letter? At any rate, when we read the above extracts, taken in their connection, and without omitting important qualifications, we find no ground whatever for concluding that Dinwiddie was conniving with Lord Loudoun or that he was unfair to Washington or even " ambiguous and uncertain." To make Governor Dinwiddie's case still stronger, we find that he says in a letter [81] to Washington, November 16, 1756, concerning Lord Loudoun's attitude to him and his letters: " I have repeatedly wrote Lord Loudoun of the Necessity of an Offensive War and Expedition to the Ohio . . . but no Answer." This does not look like close relations and an opportunity for conniving!

---

[80] Ford, Writings of Washington, vol. i, p. 312.
[81] Dinwiddie Papers, vol. ii, p. 552.

6

It may be startling to read words like the following to Washington from any pen: " I can not agree to allow you Leave to come down at this Time; you have been frequently indulged with Leave of Absence." But he adds: " Surely the Commanding Officer should not be absent when daily alarm'd with the Enemy's Intent's to invade our frontier. I think you are wrong to ask it." This explanation takes the sting out of the first part. Furthermore, if Washington had been in Dinwiddie's shoes with the frontier in jeopardy, and a young officer of twenty-five had asked leave to go to a distant city to " settle some account," would Washington have acted differently from the way Dinwiddie acted?

The pith of much of this criticism of Dinwiddie's blunt candor in his letters to Washington comes from reading his letters in the light of what we now know of Washington, and the reverence we have for his character. Historians and biographers have thought and written of Dinwiddie as though they demanded that he span the half century in which he was living, see Washington first as the successful leader of the American colonial troops, then as first president of the new Republic, and finally as one idealized to such an extent that an early biographer of Washington's felt that he dare not publish Washington's letters without " doctoring " them to suit his own taste.[82] Surely, to expect Dinwiddie to know all of this was expecting too much of even a shrewd Scotchman! To Dinwiddie, at this time, Washington was an officer of " great Merit and Resolution," who owed his opportunities and commissions to the very man who wrote so frankly to him. And we know that Governor Dinwiddie exacted of Washington nothing more than he exacted of himself. The governor was almost a literalist in his strict adherence to the commands of men over him. When the men above the governor happened to be such incompetents as Lord Loudoun,[83] is it to be expected that commands to Washington,

[82] Jared Sparks.
[83] " Like another Fabius," as Richard Bland said in 1756 (S. M. Hamilton, Letters to Washington, vol. i, p. 394).

through a man who was himself under authority, should not
at times be conflicting?

The letter that Dinwiddie wrote to Washington charging
him with ingratitude, is pathetic rather than blameworthy,
if read in the light of the facts. Washington had supposed
that Dinwiddie had been misrepresenting him to Lord Loudoun; he supposed that the ambiguous orders he was receiving were the results of incompetence or want of stability on
the governor's part. Washington had allowed himself to
become estranged from Dinwiddie, not from any fault in
Washington, as we now see it, but because there were insin-
uating men at work who took advantage of the situations
of the two men and sought to make a breach where tempera-
ment had already made such a thing easy. Hence the mis-
understandings which are referred to by Dinwiddie in one
of his last letters to Washington. The governor's sincerity
is so obvious and his appeal to Washington's conscience is
so unusual, that we can not doubt that Dinwiddie was much
hurt by what he took to be want of appreciation on the part
of Washington. Under date of September 24, 1757, he
wrote Washington:

My Conduct to Yo. from the Beginning was always Friendly, but
Yo. know I had g't Reason to suspect Yo. of Ingratitude, w'ch I am
convinc'd your own Conscience and reflec'n must allow I had Reason
to be angry, but this I endeavor to forget; . . . However, as I have
his Majesty's Leave to go for England, I propose leaving this in
Nov'r, and I wish my Successor may show Yo. as much Friendship
as I've done.[84]

Taking into consideration the broken health of Dinwiddie,
and the youth of Washington, considering also how false
had been the accusation that Dinwiddie was in any sense
inimical to Washington, and how hard Dinwiddie had tried
to be just to the many men who claimed rights above him to
speak and act, leaving the governor to reconcile their conflicting commands as best he could—we believe we do by
Governor Dinwiddie what Washington would do were he
in our stead and with all the facts before him. The great

---

[84] Dinwiddie Papers, vol. ii, p. 703.

Virginian was too magnanimous to be unjust to a loyal, sincere, overworked old man, who was trying amidst bodily enfeeblement to do his full duty to his country and to perform a task that was too much for his strength and his powers. We, on the other hand, believe that Washington would have been the first to subscribe to the following appreciation of Governor Dinwiddie, passed April 16, 1757, by the Council at Williamsburg:

The Toil and Labor that you have undergone in the Service of Your King and Country, were never experienc'd by any of Your Predecessors. When You retire from the Fatigue of Business, You will feel the Satisfaction arising from Your past Conduct and the Virtues of the good Citizen will then stand eminently distinguished, and receive Lustre from Your public Character.[85]

A summary of the events for the period we have just spoken of will now be given. Washington was allowed to appoint as his subordinate officers Lieutenant-Colonel Adam Stephen, and Major Andrew Lewis. Of these two men, Lewis, who had quite a romantic career as an Indian fighter, finally became brigadier-general in the Revolutionary War. He was regarded as such a distinct type of American soldier, that his statue was placed among the six representatives of the early days of our country, upon the base of the statue of Washington at Richmond, Virginia.

After taking steps to organize the regiment, Washington went at once to Winchester, which he made his headquarters. Notwithstanding the fact that the governor and the assembly seem to have granted so much to Washington, when he came to put into practice the powers that had been accorded him, he found that his troubles had just begun. Judging by the character of letters Washington wrote to Dinwiddie and to others during this period, his mind must have been agitated at times almost to desperation. We have spoken before of the individualistic character of the frontiersmen of this period, particularly of the Scotch-Irish. This people had very largely settled the mountainous sections of the frontier with which Washington now had to

---

[85] Ibid., vol. ii, p. 614.

do. Such men were not easily brought under the control of rigid military discipline. The settlers of one county had little community feeling for the settlers of another. The people of Frederick actually said when appealed to by the people of Hampshire to help them in their attempts against the Indians, " Let Hampshire take care of itself as we will do if we are attacked." The Germans who occupied the lower Shenandoah Valley insisted on keeping to themselves and speaking their own language.[86] The assembly of Virginia had provided for a heavy enlistment, but the legal exemptions [87] were so many and it was so easy to purchase exemption (by the payment of £10) that many took advantage of this opportunity to escape enlistment. This left Washington to gather from the lowest classes of citizens whatever he could to make up an army.

Those historians who make merry over the character of Washington's soldiers do not always say what he made out of them and what they accomplished. Concerning these very men whom Washington had trained, the officers of this army could say of the men early in 1760 that "by close application and steady perseverance in the punctual execution of their duty, such good order, regularity, and strict discipline have long been maintained in the regiment,[88] so as to attract the particular notice and approbation of the best judges, and to acquire a superiority over all other provincial troops." [89] Indian raids continued [90] all along the border. Savages poured in particularly in the neighborhood of Fort Cumberland and through the mountain passes into

[86] Ibid., vol. i, p. 406.

[87] Some 8,000 exemptions in a militia list of 43,329 (Dinwiddie Papers, vol. ii, p. 476). The Act of Assembly allowed a person drafted to pay £10 and escape service. The result was that most of the drafts paid the fine and the companies remained unfilled (Ford, Writings of Washington, vol. i, p. 299n).

[88] For a list of the officers in the Virginia regiment, July 12, 1756, see Hamilton, vol. i, pp. 297-300.

[89] Journals, 1758-1761, p. 162.

[90] Richard Bland, in 1756, refers to Fort Duquesne as "that Source from whence all our present Evils flow" (Hamilton, vol. i, p. 394).

Augusta County. Due to the weakness of the laws [91] governing soldiers and to the difficulties of enlisting men,[92] just referred to, Washington found he could not hold the Indians in check. The year 1755-1756 will go down in history as one of the most memorable and murderous in connection with American frontier life.

Two distinct expeditions stand out as connected with the Virginia Frontier, or at least, with the men associated with the frontier about this time. The first of these is known as the Sandy Creek Expedition [93] under the command of Major Andrew Lewis and was directed against the Shawmee Indians on the Ohio. It was somehow badly managed and resulted [94] in the loss [95] of men, supplies and prestige.[96]

At the time of this expedition, Washington made his first tour to the North, to lay certain matters before Governor Shirley who, after the death of Braddock, was commander-in-chief of the American forces. A certain Captain Dagworthy, who held a royal commission and who was at

---

[91] And to make matters much worse, the government was restrained from marching any part of the "militia, or causing them to be marched, more than five Miles beyond where the Inhabitants of this Colony shall be settled on the Western Frontier. . . ." "If the Officers attempt to lead them [the militia] further, the men may, legally, refuse to obey. . . ." "As the Inhabitants abandon the Frontiers . . . very fast, the Officers are more and more circumscribed in their Boundaries " (Hamilton, vol. i, pp. 392-393).

[92] For the pay (in shillings and in tobacco) of officers and enlisted men, see Hening, vol. vi, p. 116; Hamilton, vol. i, p. 28, giving minutes of a council of war, April 27, 1754; Washington, MSS., Library of Congress, vol. i, pp. 29-30, " A Pay Roll of the Virginia Regiment. . . ."

[93] February-April, 1756, Draper, MSS., 1U1ff; 1QQ96-123 (Preston's Journal); Captain Hog to Washington, April 3, 1756, Hamilton, vol. i, pp. 207-208; Dinwiddie to Captains Preston and Smith, December 15, 1755, Draper, MSS., 1QQ90; Colonel Lewis to Captain Preston, January 28, 1756, Draper, MSS., 1QQ94.

[94] Colonel Pendleton to Captain Preston, May 12, 1756, Draper, MSS., 1QQ126-128; Dinwiddie to Preston, April 24, 1756 (ibid., MSS., 1QQ125); Minutes of a council of war, April 27, 1754 (Hamilton, vol. i, p. 28).

[95] Captain Preston to Governor Dinwiddie, April 8, 1756, Draper, MSS., 1QQ124.

[96] Such failures were always followed by serious Indian irruptions upon the frontiers. One occurred in April, 1756 (Campbell, pp. 492-493; Hamilton, vol. i, pp. 216, 220, 223, 239, 270, 308, 325).

this time associated with others at Fort Cumberland, disputed Washington's right to a command over him. Governor Sharpe of Maryland, always disposed to be fair, seems this time to have sided with Captain Dagworthy—influenced somewhat in his feeling by the fact that Fort Cumberland was on Maryland territory and, therefore, not under the control of a man whose command was limited to the forces of Virginia. Governor Dinwiddie, who espoused the cause of Washington, could not enforce obedience upon Captain Dagworthy. To settl. this question [97] once for all, Washington went to Boston to see Governor Shirley. Authorities tell us that he went accompanied by two other officers, all of them dressed in gay uniforms, and having with them their colored servants. In addition to seeing Governor Shirley, Washington seems to have made a great impression upon the people of the North. He was hailed as the "Hero of the Monongahela." The press gave notice of his presence as he came and went on his journey to and from Massachusetts. Is it too much to venture that the impression that Washington made upon the people of the far North on this journey had considerable to do with his being the choice of the Philadelphia convention in 1775, when they made him commander-in-chief of the colonial forces of the Revolutionary War? It was John Adams of Massachusetts who made the ringing speech on that occasion in favor of Washington, which probably settled the question of his selection. Adams saw that Washington was "a man of independent fortune" as well as a man of experience in handling troops—and by far the most popular soldier in that day, both North and South,—hence the lot fell upon him to be the great captain of the Revolution.

Having had the matter of his authority over such men as Dagworthy settled, and having received inspiration from what was almost an ovation on his way to and from Massachusetts, Washington threw himself anew into the matter

---

[97] He set out February 4, 1756 (Ford, Writings of Washington, vol. i, pp. 230-234; Sparks, vol. i, p. 77; Campbell, p. 487).

of protecting the Virginia Frontier by appealing to the assembly at Williamsburg, and by working in conjunction with Dinwiddie on a scheme of fortifying [98] the frontier by a series of forts, stockades, and block-houses. A list of these forts will be given later with details as to where they were built, when they were built, and why they were built. Suffice it to say here that this plan to fortify the frontier and by this means to enable a small garrison in connection with the settlers round about the fortification to protect themselves, was one of the most important acts of Governor Dinwiddie's entire administration. There was some difference of opinion between Washington and Governor Dinwiddie as to the number and location of forts, but in the main they were together in the scheme as a whole.

Governor Dinwiddie retired from his position as chief executive of the Virginia colony late in the year 1757. About this time Washington was taken very ill and had to retire to Mount Vernon where for months he was confined to his bed and in a very weakened condition. When he again appeared upon the scene of action the famous Forbes expedition was gathering momentum and he was able to take part in it. This enterprise against Fort Duquesne is unique in the history of campaigns in that it partook of the nature of wearing out the enemy by forcing them to wait an interminable time for an attack. With a force of over six thousand men, and consuming five months to reach the Forks of the Ohio, Forbes, on November 26, 1758, "took

---

[98] The Preston Papers for 1756, and particularly for 1757, abound with entries concerning the building and garrisoning of forts; for example, Lewis to Dinwiddie, Fort Vaux, June, 1756 (Draper, MSS. 1QQ131-132); Lewis to Preston, Miller's and Wilson's forts, November 23, 1756 (ibid., 1QQ137; ibid., fort in Bull Pasture, February 26, 1757 (ibid., 1QQ150-151); ibid., March 7, 1757 (ibid., 1QQ147); William Ralston, Statement of account against "The Country" for provisions delivered "at Fort William in Augusta," March 22, 1757 (ibid., 1QQ146); Robert Hall, receipt to Captain Preston for 27s for twenty-seven days' service at Fort Lewis, August 4, 1757 (ibid., 6QQ68); Robert Knox to Preston, receipt for 9s for nine days' work at Fort George, September 20, 1757 (ibid., 6QQ20); Charles Campbell to Preston, October 11, 1757, receipt for 5s 6d for a spade used in building Fort George (ibid., 6QQ22).

possession of Fort Duquesne, or rather the place where it had stood.[99]

The order of events was as follows: In the summer of 1758 General Forbes was ordered by General Amherst, who then had command of the American forces, to undertake a campaign against Fort Duquesne. Forbes had in all, between six and seven thousand men. Of these about two thousand were Virginians,[100] among them Major Andrew Lewis and Captain Thomas Bullitt, each commanding a small number of men. It would have been the natural thing for General Forbes to follow the Braddock route to Fort Duquesne, and Washington, as colonel of the First Virginia Regiment, advised this course. But for some reason General Forbes elected to cut a new way through the forest, and to fortify his way as he went. There is a suggestion in General Forbes' refusal to follow the Braddock route that he was superstitious about it. It had already been the route of several expeditions that had failed. Anyhow, the course Forbes took by way of Raystown, Loyal Hanna, and Fort Ligonier, consumed so much time that winter was upon him before he was in the proximity of Fort Duquesne. The only actual attempt against the enemy, by any of his men, was made by Major Grant, who pushed ahead with eight hundred men to reconnoitre and was ambushed, losing [101] half his force—among them Major Lewis who was captured. Forbes seems to have become dispirited and would have recalled his forces for the winter, but by good fortune he learned from some prisoners that the Indians who had been with the French at the fort had become disgusted with waiting for General Forbes to make an attack and had deserted the French. Thus the French were so weak that an attack of almost any sort would have been successful. Washington with his regiment pushed on to the fort to find it disbanded and destroyed. Thus General

---

[99] Sparks, p. 101.
[100] Draper, MSS., 4ZZ41-53; Journals, 1758-1761, pp. 261-266.
[101] William Fleming's list of "kild and missing in Grant's engagement," Sept. 14, 1758 (Draper, MSS., 3ZZ48).

Forbes took the Gibraltar of the Mountains! The British at once began the construction of a new fort which they appropriately called Fort Pitt, after the strong man who was at the helm of affairs in the Mother Country.

The fall of Fort Duquesne, which had been a base for Indian supplies and raids since 1754, was the most pronounced turn in affairs for the good of the Virginia Frontier that had as yet been effected. Duquesne had been the scene of Trent's defeat, of Washington's capitulation, and Braddock's disaster. It had meant humiliation, death, and almost despair to the people of the Virginia colony. Governor Dinwiddie, even though now in England, must have breathed a thankful prayer when he knew that at last this Gateway to the West was in the control of the British, and that the force left to command the new fort was composed of Washington's men.

Washington's direct connection with the defense of the frontier as a soldier now came to an end. He soon afterwards married Mrs. John Parke Custis, celebrated for her beauty, wit, and wealth. Matters now began to take definite shape and the cruel years that Dinwiddie and he had suffered together were beginning to yield a harvest. Pitt was prime minister in England; the fall of Quebec was close at hand; and Washington had been elected [102] in the meantime as a member of the house of burgesses. Washington had now a breathing spell before he was to assume his task as commander-in-chief of all the colonial forces of America in their war for independence.

Notwithstanding the service that Washington rendered his country in that great war, and notwithstanding what he did for the young Republic as its first president, it is doubtful whether he ever did or ever could render again such service as he gave America in the French and Indian War. Washington saw from the first, with Dinwiddie, that the Ohio Valley was the key to the possession of the North American continent, and that Fort Duquesne was the key to the Ohio Valley,—hence to lose that fort or to hold that fort meant to

---

[102] From the County of Frederick.

lose or to hold the continent of America. As this fortification was supposedly at that time within the territory of Virginia, and as the contest waged about that fort, and as Virginians felt that it was their task to take this place in behalf of the British government,—we assert that the Virginia Frontier and the Virginia soldiers saw the most important operations connected with the French and Indian War.

CHAPTER V

THE CLOSING YEARS OF THE WAR

The course of events in the French and Indian War up to 1757 has been very well described by Doctor Lyman C. Draper in a hitherto unpublished manuscript:

The war had thus far (1757) resulted disastrously to the English cause,—driven from the Ohio Valley; compelled to surrender Fort Necessity; overwhelmingly defeated at Monongahela; Fort William on Lake George carried and its garrison inhumanly massacred; frontier posts in New York, Pennsylvania and Virginia taken, their inmates butchered, burned, or hopelessly captivated; well-digested campaigns miscarried; the whole northern frontier, by swarming bands of French and Indians, rendered almost one continuous scene of unexampled terror and desolation. General William Johnson had gained a victory over Dieskau, and Colonel John Armstrong made a successful expedition against Kittanning; all else wore an aspect sad and gloomy. But in 1758, the salutary effect of Pitt's new administration began to be powerfully felt, as well in Great Britain as the colonies; new life and energy were infused into every department. Expeditions wisely planned, were vigorously executed. Louisburg, Frontenac and Duquesne successfully fell into the hands of the victorious English, and their only check was that of Abercrombie at Ticonderoga. These fortunate results paved the way for the capture of Niagara and Quebec the following year, and the ultimate conquest of all Canada; and with it, the final downfall of French power and dominion in North America.[1]

About the time the colonists thought that all war clouds had been completely swept away, a sudden storm burst upon them like a hurricane from the gulf regions, striking the southwestern frontier of Virginia and the western portions of the Carolinas. This outbreak is known in history as the Cherokee War. Fortunately, it was handled wisely and was, as a consequence, short-lived. This war against the Indians was confined almost entirely to Virginia and the Carolinas.

The facts concerning the cause of the war are about as follows: A body of Cherokees, early in 1758, joined Colonel Washington at Winchester, with a view to taking part in General Forbes' projected campaign against Fort Duquesne. As we have seen, General Forbes was slow in his movements against the fort and the Indians from the Cherokee tribe be-

[1] Draper, MSS., 2B69-70.

came impatient and returned home.[2] On their way home, in passing through the Virginia colony, they were thoughtlessly guilty of some depredations in the way of horse-stealing. The colonists [3] without taking into consideration the easy morals of the Indians, fell upon the offenders and killed quite a number. The surviving Indians consequently went back to their homes in a very bad mood and war would have broken out immediately but for the timely action of Governor Lyttleton of South Carolina who temporarily appeased the Indians and thus, for the time, prevented an outbreak.

A new element now entered. Certain Frenchmen, after the fall of Fort Duquesne, made their way to the South and finding the Cherokee Indians somewhat alienated from their English neighbors, began a propaganda [4] of anti-British feeling, and were able to make a treaty with the Cherokees. When Governor Lyttleton made his treaty with these Indians he had stipulated that they should surrender to the English certain bad Indians that had been foremost in making trouble in connection with the Forbes expedition. The Indians agreed to do this and in testimony of their good faith had left a number of their warriors as hostages at Fort Prince George, in South Carolina. After the forces of South Carolina had been withdrawn from the region of the fort, the Indians made an attack upon it in order to rescue the men whom they had left as hostages. The garrison of the fort, disgusted and enraged at such treachery, killed the men that were held as hostages. Taking into consideration the strained relations that had existed between the Cherokees and the English colonists, augmented largely by French influence, the killing of their warriors held as hostages was the last straw. Indian hatred burst forth in all its fury, and the war was on.

---

[2] Ibid., 2B70-71, referring to Virginia Gazette, May 26, 1758; Hewitt's Historical Account in Carroll's Collection, vol. i, p. 443; Joseph Martin, North Carolina, vol. ii, p. 97.

[3] Captain Wade and a party, letter of Governor Fauquier, Nov. 14, 1758, Draper, MSS., 2B72; Calendar of Virginia State Papers, vol. i, p. 258.

[4] Draper, MSS., 2B72, 94, 98, referring to Maryland Gazette, May 24, June 21, July 5, 1759, November 27, 1760, and Pennslyvania Gazette, July 9, 1761.

As a natural consequence, the Indians invested Fort Loudoun. This fort had been built by Major Andrew Lewis of Virginia in 1756 in the Cherokee Indian country, at the request of the Cherokees themselves, and was now garrisoned by two hundred British troops. It stood on the Holston River about thirty miles south of present Knoxville, Tennessee, and was in those days, supposed to be on Virginia soil. The Virginia assembly, on hearing of the danger to the fort, acted with decision. It voted (March, 1760) to maintain the Virginia regiment in the field until November 1, 1760, and also agreed to maintain three companies of one hundred men each to keep watch over the western frontier. The May (1760) session of the assembly, hastily called, immediately authorized the raising of seven hundred men to be joined with the three hundred already on the border in the southwest, which combined force should make its way to the relief of Fort Loudoun. Unfortunately, the seven hundred men provided for were not raised, and the military forces to be used consisted only of the troops already in the field. The assembly voted, however, to retain in the service the men in the field until December, 1760, and allowed the governor to send them, if necessary, outside the province.

Colonel Montgomery, acting under orders from General Amherst, now commander-in-chief of the British forces in America, with a small army of British regulars and Carolinians sought out the Indians, defeated them in a pitched battle, and then relieved Fort Prince George. He abandoned, however, the attempt to raise the siege of Fort Loudoun. This fort's brave garrison was, therefore, doomed,—as the Virginians under Colonel William Byrd were never able to force their way to its rescue,—and was massacred in cold blood, even though it had capitulated on a promise of safe-conduct to the East.

General Amherst, during the winter of 1760-1761, arranged with the governors of Virginia and North and South Carolina a plan of campaign.[5] Colonel James Grant, uniting a force

---

[5] Correspondence of General Jeffery Amherst to Governors Francis Fauquier, of Virginia, William Bell, of South Carolina, Arthur Dobbs,

of British regulars and South Carolina provincials, was to move to the attack on the Lower and Middle Cherokee towns; Colonel William Byrd, with the provincials of Virginia and North Carolina, was to proceed at the same time down the Clinch and Tennessee Rivers and make an attack on the Cherokee " Over Hill " towns,—the towns beyond the mountains, in the valley of the Tennessee River. Grant succeeded [6] in his attempt. Colonel Byrd,[7] however, with six hundred men, took up most of his time building forts and roads, following somewhat the tactics of General Forbes on his way to Fort Duquesne. The soldiers became dissatisfied and Colonel Byrd resigned in disgust; his place was taken by Colonel Adam Stephen. So much time having been already spent, Colonel Stephen marched rapidly to the Long Island of Holston, about one hundred miles from the enemy's settlements, and began the construction of a fort on the river near the Long Island, in compliance with Governor Fauquier's instructions. Before this fort, which was called Fort Robinson, was completed, a satisfactory peace was made with the Cherokees, November 19, 1760. Thus ended the Cherokee War.

The Virginia regiment was for a short time reconstituted by the March assembly of 1762, when the news was received that England had declared war on Spain. A regiment of one thousand men was held on the western frontier until order was given to disband the force in May, 1763. " It broke up just when needed," says Eckenrode,[8] " for in 1763 the Indians

---

of North Carolina, and Colonel William Byrd, of Virginia, regarding the campaign, Draper, MSS., 4ZZ26, 33, 35-39, 46-49, 54, 56; Journals, 1758-1761, pp. 266-280. Fauquier was successor to Dinwiddie, 1758.

[6] Draper, MSS., 2B98-103.

[7] General Jeffery Amherst to Colonel William Byrd, and Byrd to Amherst, July-August, 1761, Draper, MSS., 4ZZ33, 36, 37-39, 56; Journals, 1758-1761, pp. 278-280; Draper, MSS., 2B92, referring to South Carolina Gazette, October 18, 1760, Maryland Gazette, April 3, November 6, 20, December 24, 1760, and to Timberlake's Memoirs, p. 6. Colonel William Byrd of " Westover," James River, the third of the name, was county-lieutenant of Halifax county, member of the council, and colonel of the Second Virginia Regiment. He died January 1, 1777, aged 48 years (R. A. Brock, Dinwiddie Papers, vol. ii, p. 110n.).

of the whole frontier, acting with a unity they never attained before or afterwards, attacked the British posts from Mackinaw to Fort Pitt, laying waste the settlements in New York, Maryland, and Virginia.[9] The Virginia regiment had been disbanded because the board of trade would not allow the colony to issue the paper money needed for its maintenance, but in August, 1763, the governor and council called out one thousand militia from Hampshire and the adjoining counties, half of them under the command of Colonel Adam Stephen and half under Major Andrew Lewis, both of whom were now officers of the best quality."

The war spoken of here is known in history as Pontiac's War. It followed after the formal closing of the French and Indian War. The fall of Quebec practically closed the French and Indian War, but it was not officially terminated until the Peace of Paris in 1763. Pontiac's War does not come within the purview of this study, but it has practical bearings on the Virginia Frontier too important to be left unnoticed. Although this was the most concerted movement that the Indians had ever attempted against the English colonists, and the movement was led by the most capable and ambitious of the Indian leaders—Pontiac—still, two elements entered into the contest which rendered the defeat of the Indians certain. The first of these was, the Indians lacked cooperation and the leadership of their former French allies; the second was the character of the fortifications which the Indians had to overcome in order to reach the heart of the English colonies. Here the fine work of Dinwiddie and Washington will be noted for the last time. The Virginia Frontier was so effectively fortified that with anything like a force garrisoning the fortifications, such an attack as Pontiac made, even if he had thrown his whole force against them, was bound to be unsuccessful.

As matters stood, Colonel Bouquet, with five hundred men, at the old strategic point, which had now been called Fort

---

[8] H. J. Eckenrode, List of Colonial Soldiers of Virginia, p. 13.

[9] William Fleming to Governor Fauquier, July 26, 1763, reporting the general consternation brought about by the invasion of Augusta (Draper, MSS., 3ZZ50-51).

Pitt, was able to defeat the Indians, August 5-6, 1763; and later, with 1,500 men, he marched into the Ohio country and compelled the Indians to sue for peace. Pontiac demurred, hoping for aid from the French, but he finally gave in, though unwillingly, at Oswego in 1766. So aggressive had become the Virginia Frontier and so far had it pushed westward at the time of which we now write that in the famous battle of Point Pleasant which took place in 1774, where Colonel Andrew Lewis completely routed the Indians, he had to penetrate the frontier as far as the Ohio River in order to reach the enemy.

Virginia, as well as the other colonies, was now practically safe from concerted Indian attacks. They had their forces so well in hand, and their leaders so ably developed that they could turn a united front to meet the forces of the Mother Country, defeat those forces, and after eight years of war under the leadership of Washington, actually win their independence.

CHAPTER VI

THE FORTS ON THE FRONTIER

The English nation has always been strong in defense. Once having taken an advanced position and fortified it, the British instinct is to hold it to the bitter end. In line with this trait of national character, Governor Dinwiddie of Virginia saw from the very first that the extended frontier of the colony must be fortified at strategic points. He outlined a plan [1] which finally resulted in a cordon of forts, stockades, and block-houses which stretched along the entire frontier [2] of Virginia, joining the colonies to the North and to the South, thus fortifying the outposts of the English settlements from Crown Point, New York, to the borders of Georgia. The mind of Dinwiddie and the hand of Washington manifested themselves in the fact that the Virginia Frontier was literally dotted with these fortifications, while the frontiers of the other colonies North and South were meagerly defended. There was some difference of opinion between Governor Dinwiddie and Washington as to the number of forts, but as the following letter will show, the governor left that matter largely to Washington:

Sir:

Your L're of the 4th I rec'd and note its Contents. I observe you have been much engag'd in settling the proper Places for the Chain of Forts propos'd to be built, and I doubt not the Places you have pitched upon are the most proper, as you know the Situation of the Country, you are the best Judge thereof. . . .   The

---

[1] Dinwiddie presented his plan to the British Lords of Trade in February, 1756. He proposed to pay for the building of the forts and the maintenance of their garrisons by a land and poll tax, levied on all the colonies by act of Parliament (Dinwiddie Papers, vol. i, pp. 96-97, vol. ii, pp. 338-346, 406-408, 434-435, 460-461, 478-483; Ford, Writings of Washington, vol. i, p. 261n.). Dinwiddie indeed as early as June 16, 1753, submitted a tentative proposal to the king (Loudoun Papers, Dinwiddie file, 1753, Aug. 28; see above, Chap. iv, n. 39.

[2] Although a few of the forts were standing as early as 1754 and 1755, most of them were built about 1756, and continued to do service until the end of the war; some of them stood until many years afterward; see Appendix II, Nos. 1, 8.

building of Forts is a necessary work, but the protecting of the Frontier is more essential, therefore I w'd recommend as much as you possibly can to have Y'r Men at Call on any approaching Danger, tho' I fear it will be impracticable when divided at such a Distance, unless you appoint a proper Place for a general Rendeswouse on proper Alarms given w'ch you are the only Judge of from y'r Knowledge of the Country. . . . I have order'd three Forts in Halifax and one in Bedford to be built by the Militia and Garrison'd by them some time.

S'r, y'r mo. h'ble Serv't [3]

The governor and Washington agreed on this one principle, namely, that a fortification built far out on the frontier had the advantage of inducing the people to venture farther westward [4] from the more congested sections of the colony. This leading of the people out towards the West served the purpose of having more of the territory taken up by hardy frontiersmen who acted both as an advance guard to protect the more eastern sections and as a friendly vanguard in dealing with the Indians.

The defenses on the Virginia Frontier were of three classes, —block-houses, stockades, and forts. The block-houses were simple, two storied, log buildings, and square, having the second story projecting beyond the lower. There were numerous rifle holes through the logs so that the defenders could fire down upon assailants without great danger of being themselves hit by return shots. The stockade—a kind of fort with palisade—was much stronger than the blockhouse. It was usually a double-log structure, two stories in height, surrounded at a distance by a high fence of stakes driven into the ground. The forts were the most pretentious of the fortifications, combining as a rule the features of both the other kinds of buildings. They were generally rectangular, having block-houses at the four corners and these connected by a palisaded fence. The doors of the block-houses opened into the inner court.

The stockades and forts were more than posts for garrisons; they were the places of refuge to which the people in the vicinity of the forts flocked, and in which they sought

---

[3] Written August 9, 1756 (Dinwiddie Papers, vol. ii, pp. 479-483).
[4] Ford, Writings of Washington, vol. i, pp. 260-261.

shelter when Indians made attacks in the neighborhood. At one time, in 1756, the ravages of the Indians were having such a demoralizing effect on the frontier that Washington suggested that the people on the frontier be compelled to group themselves together into villages, very much after the manner of the French farm villages of today.

As an outcome of Dinwiddie's agitation of the matter of frontier defense, an act was passed in March, 1756, at the first session of the new assembly of 1756-1758, which provided " that a chain of forts shall be erected, to begin at Henry Enochs, on Great-Cape-Capon, in the county of Hampshire, and to extend to the South-Fork of Mayo-River, in the county of Halifax, to consist of such a number, and at such distance from each other, as shall be thought necessary and directed by the governor, or commander in chief of this colony, for the time being. . . ." [5]   The responsibility for the building of these forts fell ultimately upon Washington.

In pursuance of the authorization by the Virginia assembly in March, 1756, for the building of the cordon of forts, a council of war was called at Augusta Court House,[6] July 27, 1756.   The following record [7] of the council of war gives the locations of the forts, their distance from each other, and the number of men estimated to garrison each one of them.

At a Council of War held at Augusta Court House (in obedience to his Honor the Governors Orders). By the undernamed Officers.

PRESENT

Col. John Buchanan & David Stewart.
Major John Brown

Captains	Joseph Culton	James Lockart
	Robert Scott	Israel Christian
	Patrick Martin	Samuel Stalnicker
	Wm. Christian	Thomas Armstrong
	Robert Breckenridge	

Who having taken their seats proceeded to business.

Whereas his Honor the Governor has sent repeated orders to

---

[5] Hening, vol. vii, pp. 17-18.
[6] Now Staunton, Virginia, where the first court in Augusta County was held, 1745.
[7] For the complete record see Appendix I. Not all of the forts authorized were actually built.

the officers of the Militia of this country to meet and consult on the most proper Places to build forts along the Frontiers for the Protection of the inhabitants. . . .

It is agreed that the following numbers of men is necessary to be placed at each fort.

	Men	
At Mason's Fort	30	
at Vances (Fort Vass)	70	
at Campbell's Fort	50	
at McNeal's Fort	30	
at Fort William	50	exclusive of
at John's Creek	50	Officers
at Capt. Deekens (Dickensons) Fort	40	
at Capt. Brackenridge Fort	50	
at Capt. Miller's Fort	50	
at Harper's Fort	50	
at Trout Rock Fort	50	
at Hugh Man's Mill	50	
at Petersons	50	
Dinwiddie	60	

680 Men in all to
protect ye frontiers.

It is agreed that the commanding officers give orders that Fort Vanse (Vass) be made at least one hundred feet square in the clear; and that the stockades be at least fourteen feet long; that all the other forts be made 60 feet square with two bastions in each fort, provided the same be agreeable to Capt. Peter Hog, who is supposed to have His Honor, the Governor's Orders to oversee the Constructing of the said chain of forts. The distance between each fort above mentioned, or the place agreed for them to be built, on, are as follows (viz)

	Miles
From the County Line to Peterson's	2
From Peterson's to Hugh Man's Mill	18
from thence to Trout Rock	17
From Trout Rock to Mathew Harper's	20
from thence to Capt. Miller's	18
from thence to Fort Dinwiddie	15
from thence to Capt. Brackenridge's Fort	13
from thence to Fort Dickenson	13
from thence to John's Creek	25
from thence to Fort William	20
From Fort William to Neal McNeal's	13
From thence to Capt. Campbell's	13
From thence to Capt. Vances (Vass's)	12
From thence to John Mason's	20

From thence to the first Inhabitants in   250 miles in all.
    Halifax County South side of Ridge.
        By which we find our Frontiers ex-
            tend.

The above resolves are signed by all the Officers present this 27 day of July 1756.

John Buchanan
David Stewart
John Brown
Joseph Culton
Robert Scott
James Lockart
Israel Christian
Wm. Christian
James Mitchell
Robert Brackenridge
Thomas Armstrong
Pattrick Martin
Samuel Stalnacker [8]

TEST:
    Wm. Preston, Clk.
      Council of War.

In the meantime, Washington, without awaiting the decision of the Council of War at Augusta, prepared, July 21, 1756, the following letter of instructions for Captain Peter Hog,[9] of the Virginia regiment, who was to engage in building the southern section of the chain of forts. This letter very well pictures for us the nature of the task before Washington and his subordinates.

INSTRUCTIONS FOR CAPTAIN PETER HOG, OF THE VIRGINIA REGIMENT.

Sir:

As the Assembly has voted a chain of Forts to be built on the Frontiers, The Governor has ordered out the Militia of Augusta to assist you in erecting them, and it was determined in a Councile of War [10] held at Fort Cumberland, agreeable to the Governor's orders, that you should have the care of construct'g them, ' and that you should receive directions to Build at or about 20 or 30 miles distance, as the situation of the Country requires, or Ground will permit, and to have particular regard to the Body of Inhabitants to be defended, and, the passes most frequented by the Enemy, and that Capt. Hog begin to build, observing the above considerations, to the Southward of Fort Dinwiddie, extending the Line towards Mayo River as directed by the Assembly.'

You are, therefore, as soon as possible, to proceed to Augusta Court-house and consult with the Comanding Officers, and others of that County, and fall upon the most expeditious methods to raise the Militia, with which and Your own Company, except about

---

[8] Virginia Magazine of History, vol. xv (pp. 247-251, 1907-1908; Hamilton, vol. i, pp. 305-307.

[9] Captain Hog already had had experience in building forts; for example, see his letter to Washington from Fort Dinwiddie, November 29, 1755 (Hamilton, vol. i, pp. 137-138).

[10] Held October 30, 1756 (Ford, Writings of Washington, vol. i, p. 364).

30 private wh. you are to leave under the Command of Lt. Bullet, at Fort Dinwiddie, and set immediately upon that Duty, taking Care also to observe the orders herewith sent you by His Honor, the Governor, and to draft the best Work men to take with you.

If you are apprehensive that the Enemy will annoy you, and endeavour to obstruct your erecting these Forts, You are first to proceed to the place which shall be judged most convenient for the defense of the Inhabitants, and Erect your first Fort there—if not—proceed as first directed.

You are, while upon this Work, to keep out constant covering parties, and above all things guard against a surprize.

I have sent you herewith a plan of the kind of Forts you are to build, which you must follow exactly.

The men drafted from your Company for this comand will receive double pay for every day they work, wh. you are to be exact in taking account of, 'tis the Same that's allowed the soldiers here who work, and the Militia will receive 6d. extra for every day they work.[11]   Both Soldiers and Militia here are contented w'h this allowance.

I hope your own Company with the Addition of the Militia, will be sufficient force to conduct this work, but lest dividing your Men may subject your separated partys to the insult of the Enemy, I wou'd have you keep in a Body and Build Fort after Fort, leaving Garrisons in them from 15 to 30 men under comand of a sub or Trusty Sergeant.

As the Difficulty of getting Tools in these parts is not easily to be conceived, I would advise you to pursue the same methods in Augusta that I have done here, vizt., to get of the Inhabitants, giving receipts for the Quantity and Sorts of Each, and paying for the use, also the damage and Loss, if any is sustain'd, but to buy wou'd be best; if this you can do, take particular care of the whole you receive.

Given under my hand, at Winches'r, 21st of July, 1756.

Go. Washington.[12]

Without much regard to the decision of the council of war held at Augusta Court House on July 27, 1756, Washington on his own initiative, in the fall of 1756, drew up the following plan for the requisite number of forts, including the

---

[11] The soldiers' pay was prescribed by Act of October, 1748 (Hening, vol. vi, p. 116), and was in tobacco. It varied for the "Horse" from 20 pounds per day which the private soldier got to 60 pounds to the colonel, and for the "Foot" from 15 pounds to the private to 50 pounds to the colonel (R. A. Brock, Dinwiddie Papers, vol. i, p. 49n.). The militia law of 1748 allowed officers and soldiers certain pay in tobacco, a colonel receiving 50, a major 40, and private 15 lbs. of tobacco a day. This proved such an awkward system that when the trouble with the French began, pay in money was allowed, as follows: colonel, 15s; lieutenant colonel, 12s, 6d; major, 10s; captain 8s; lieutenants, 4s; ensigns, 3s; surgeons, 4s; privates, 8d and a pistole on enlisting (Ford, Writings of Washington, vol. i, p. 77n.).

[12] Dinwiddie Papers, vol. ii, pp. 460-461.

size of each garrison, and the location of each fort. This plan, based upon the act of assembly of March, 1756, he thought would adequately protect the entire frontier.

LOCATION OF THE FORTS

A Plan of the Number of Forts, and strength necessary to each extending entirely across our Frontiers, from South to North.

Names of the Forts, or Persons commanding in them	On what waters Placed	Distance from each other in miles	No. of men garrisoning each
Capt. Harris	Mayo		20
Galloway	Smith's River	12	20
Terry	Black Water	26	20
Hog	Roanoke	26	150
Not built	Do at Bryants	18	50
Fort William	Catawba Bas. of James River	18	75
Not built	Craik's Creek, Bra. of Jas. River	15	40
Dickensons	Jackson's River	18	250
Brakenridge	" "	16	40
Fort Dinwiddie	" "	14	100
Christy	" "	15	40
Between this and Trout Rock—not yet built	....	18	50
Trout Rock, not built	South Branch	15	75
Upper Settlement	" "	20	60
Fort Defiance	" "	20	60
Fort Pleasant	" "	20	60
Fort at Cocke's	Patterson's Crk	20	500
Fort at Ashby's	" "	12	60
Fort at Parker's	South Branch	10	30
Enoch's, not built	Cacapehon	15	75
Maidstone	Potomack	30	125
Winchester	....	—	100
		TOTAL	2,000

This plan is calculated upon the most moderate and easy terms for sparing the county expences, and I believe with tolerable justness may answer the design of protecting the inhabitants. It may be objected that the distance between some of the forts is too small; in answer to which I must observe they are generally fixed on the heads of creeks, &c, extending towards the Alleghany Mountains with almost inaccessible mountains between them, and are placed in the most commodious manner for securing the inhabitants of such waters. Some Garrisons are larger than others, according as they cover a thick or thin settlement. The Fort at Voss's (which Capt. Hog is now building) is in a much exposed gap; subject to the inroads of the Southern Indians, and in a manner covers the greatest part of Bedford and Halifax.

Dickenson's is situated for the defense of a once numerous and fertile settlement, on the Bull Cow & Calf pastures; and lies

directly in the Shawnee path to Ohio, and must be a place of rendezvous, if an expedition is conducted against the Ohio Indians
below Duquesne.

The Garrisons on the Potomack waters, are yet larger than any;
because an invasion is most to be dreaded on this Quarter.

It will be seen Fort Cumberland is not mentioned in this plan.
If we act only on the defensive (a system on which this plan is
founded) I think it employs a large garrison to very little advantage to Virginia. If we act offensively, it may be of infinite
use, if properly fortified; and the Garrison at Cocke's will then
only consist of about 50 or 60, as the rest may be removed to
Fort Cumberland.[13]

The actual building of the series of forts involved many
problems. The work was to begin at both ends of the chain
and to proceed towards the center. It was Washington's inten-
tion, as he said, to ' visit all the ground he conveniently could,
and direct the building ' of all the forts,—he himself to
begin at the Potomac (in the late summer of 1756) and work
southward so as to meet Captain Hog who was to start at the
Mayo River at the same time and construct northward.
Washington graphically pictures some of the drawbacks that
he encountered:

It is a . . . scarcity of tools, smallness of our numbers, and
want of conductors. The strength of our forces will not admit
of many divisions, because, in that case, each party may probably
be demolished. We can, therefore, only attempt, with such men
as can be drawn out of the garrisons already established, to build
fort after fort, and not, by attempting too many at a time, thereby
run the risk of having the whole demolished. To go on in the
manner above mentioned must be extremely tedious.[14]

Washington's tours to the forts on the border inspired some
letters to Governor Dinwiddie. These letters are illuminating
to us in our day. He takes no pains to conceal the worth-
lessness of the militia, the sorrowful condition of the settlers,
and the obstacles in the way of building the forts. One letter
to the governor from Halifax (county), October 10, 1756,
continues:

We got safely to Voss's, where Captain Hog, with only eighteen
of his company, was building a fort, which must employ him until
Christmas without more assistance. One Captain Hunt from Lonen-
burg, who was there with thirty men; but none of them would

---

[13] Ford, Writings of Washington, vol. i; pp. 371-373.
[14] Ibid., pp. 287-288; see also ibid., pp. 295-296.

strike a stroke, unless I would engage to see them paid forty pounds of tobacco per day, which is provided by act of assembly for militia carpenters. This I certainly could not do, as your Honor, (who I thought had ordered them purposely out for this duty,) had given no directions in the affair. . . . The militia never lent a hand. . . .[15]

The following letter [16] from Washington to Governor Dinwiddie, written November 9, 1756, is a report on general frontier conditions as Washington saw them during his minute inspection of all the forts, and is so characteristic that we cannot do better than to give a considerable extract from it.

This jaunt, which had just been concluded, afforded me an opportunity of seeing the bad regulation of the militia, the disorderly proceedings of the garrisons, and the unhappy circumstances of the inhabitants.

I found them (the garrisons) very weak for want of men; but more so by indolence and irregularity. None I saw in a posture of defence, and few that might not be surprised with the greatest ease. An instance of this appeared at Dickinson's Fort, where the Indians ran down, caught several children playing under the walls, and had got to the gate before they were discovered. Was not Voss's Fort surprised, and a good many souls lost, in the same manner? They keep no guard, but just when the enemy is about; and are under fearful apprehensions of them; nor even stir out of the forts, from the time they reach them, till relieved on their month being expired; at which time they march off, be the event what it will. So that the neighborhood may be ravaged by the enemy, and they not the wiser. Of the ammunition they are as careless as of the provisions, firing it away frequently at targets for wagers. On our journey, as we approached one of these forts, we heard a quick fire for several minutes, and concluded for certain that they were attacked; so we marched in the best manner to their relief; but when we came up, we found they were diverting at marks. These men afford no assistance to the unhappy settlers, who are drove from their plantations, either in securing their harvests, or gathering in their corn. Lieutenant Bullett, commanding at Fort Cumberland, sent to Major Lewis of Albemarle, who commanded a party of sixty militia at Miller's, about fifteen miles above him, where were also thirty men of Augusta, for some men to join his small parties to gather the corn. Major Lewis refused assistance, and would not divide his men. I wrote to him, but got no answer. Mr. Bullett has done what he could with his few men, not quite thirty. Of the many forts, which I passed by, I saw but one or two that had their captains present, they being absent chiefly on their own business, and had given leave to several of the men to do the same. Yet these persons, I will venture to say, will charge the country their full month's pay. . . .

In the spring of 1757 the assembly having considered at

---

[15] Ibid., p. 356.   [16] Ibid., p. 379.

length " the great Expense the Virg'a Regim't has cost the
Country," completely remodelled that military organization
and placed detachments of it at selected forts on the frontier.
The governor's instructions to Washington at that time follow:

INSTRUCTIONS TO COLONEL GEORGE WASHINGTON, COM-
MANDER-IN-CHIEF OF THE VIRGINIA REGIMENT.

Sir:

You are, so soon as yo. arrive at Fort Loudoun, to inform the
Officers that the Assembly having consider'd the great Expense
the Virg'a Regim't has cost the Country from the No. of Companys it has consisted of, and those Companys not half compleat
in proportion to the vast Charge of Officers, It is resolv'd, for the
better saving of Expenses and establishing a proper Regulation,
that the said Regim't shall consist only of ten companies of 100
Men each; that all the Captains but seven be reduc'd. Those I
have thought proper to continue are Captains Mercer, Waggoner,
Stewart, Joshua Lewis, Woodward, Spotswood, and McKenzie. To
those discontinued in the Command of Captains (not from any
particular Misconduct or Demerit imputed) You are to offer Lieutenants, and compleat the No. of Lieut'ts to 20 out of the eldest
Subalterns, unless there be some whose Conduct does not entitle
'em to the Preference. The Ensigns for the Regim't are to consist of 10, and to be fill'd up in the same Manner, having regard
to their Character and Behaviour.

After the Companys are form'd You are to occupy the following Posts in the following Manner till y'r Numbers are increas'd,
Vizt:

At Fort Loudoun,	100 Men, commanded by Yourself.		
At Maidstone,	70 Men,	Do.,	by Capt. Stewart.
At Edwards'	25 Men,	Do.,	by a Subaltern.
At Persall's	45 Men,	Do.,	by Capt. McKenzie.
In the Neighborhood of Butter Milk Fort,	70 Men,	Do.,	by Capt. Waggoner.
At Dickinson's	70 Men,	Do.,	by Maj'r Lewis.
At Vass's	70 Men,	Do.,	by Capt. Woodward.

450

You are to remain at Winchester, and there use your utmost
Diligence and Care in forwarding the public Works w'th all possible Expedition.

You are to continue all the assistant Commissarys that are
requisite 'till such (time) as the Assembly comes to some futher
Resolution on this head—and issue your Orders accordingly. You
are no longer to have concern with, or Management of Indian Affairs. The Hon'ble Mr. Atkin is appointed by His M'y for that
extraordinary Service. He is now repairing to Winchester for that
purpose, and will, I suppose, if he sh'd be obliged to leave it before
the Indians return home, appoint some person to transact the Business in his absence. So soon as the Assembly have resolved on

the Ways and Means of raising Men, I shall advise you thereof, that you may be prepared for their reception, and send officers to meet them if ordered so to do.

Given at Williamsburg this 16th day of May, 1757.[17]

So critical was the situation on the frontier that Washington called a Council of War to meet at Fort Loudoun at 2 o'clock in the morning, Thursday, June 16, 1757. He had just received, he stated to the members of the council, a letter from Captain Dagworthy and another from Major James Livingston, both dated at Fort Cumberland, June 14, declaring that "a large Body of French and Indians, with a train of Artillery, were actually marched from Fort Du Quesne with a design, as they conceived, to make an attempt on Fort Cumberland." These letters he laid before the assembled group. The members present, besides Washington, were Captains Thomas Waggener, John McNeill, Robert Stewart, Christopher Gist, Lieutenants John Campbell, and Mordecai Buckner, and Ensigns William Crawford, James Roy, and Henry Russell.

The following account (was) sent to Colo. Stanwix and Governor Dinwiddie with the Council of War.

Fort Loudoun June 16th 1757.

The number of men fit for Duty in the Virginia Regiment, exclusive of the Detachment gone for Carolina—where stationed, and the distance of each Garrison from this place.

	Men			Miles
At Fort Loudoun	100	. . . .		
At Maidstone	60	Distance		36
At Edwards	15	do	. .	22
At Pearsalls	35	do	. .	50
At Fort Pleasant	30	do	. .	70
At Butter-milk Ft	28	do	. .	78
At Harness' Ft	27	do	. .	81
At Powers Mill	28	do	. .	90
At Vass's	60	do	. .	210

This reference is important not only as indicating the importance of these points but as being the only place where the distances between the forts is given.[18]

So scant is the direct information on the frontier forts and

[17] Dinwiddie Papers, vol. ii, pp. 622-623.
[18] Hamilton, vol. ii, pp. 94-96 (omitted by both Ford and Sparks).

on frontier defense that the following two fragments are important for the figures they contain.   Both are found in the Loudoun Papers.   The first is an endorsement by Lord Loudoun on a paper which reads:

Mr. Dinwiddies proposals[19] for the **Stations** (of) the **Virginia**
Troops Philadelphia March 20th 1757

        100 Men at Fort Cumberland   300 from Myld
        100 at two Stockade Forts between
            Fort Cumbld & Fort Loudoun
        150 at Fort Loudoun
        150 in Augusta Coty
        100 upon the Sea Coast
        400 for So. Carolina
        ————
        1000

The second is a mere scrap of memorandum from Sir Charles Hardy, governor of New York from 1755-1757, to the Earl of Loudoun, dated March 17, 1757, and makes reference to the garrison strength of eight of the border defenses: [20]

At Fort Cumberland	244	Rank & file
Fort Loudoun	106	Ditto
Maidstone	88	
Stephen	33	
Cocks'	41	
Pleasant	46	
Dinwiddie	50	
Pearsalls	47	

The following brief letter [21] from Governor Dinwiddie to Captain Robert Stewart, who was in command at Fort Maidstone, throws light on the conditions on the Virginia border late in 1757.   At the same time it shows the confidence that Dinwiddie continued to have in Washington.

Governor Dinwiddie to Captain Stewart.

Dec'r 9th, 1757.

Sir:

Y'rs of the 2d I rece'd, and observe its Contents.   Yo. can't possibly think it proper to go to the No'w'd unless y'r station at Fort Loudoun be duely supplied.   Maj'r Lewis can't leave his Comand in Augusta, and unless Waggoner's Fort be supplied with a proper Person I can't advise his leaving of it, and as I am a Stranger to

---

[19] Loudoun Papers, Dinwiddie file, 1757, March 20.
[20] Ibid., Hardy file, 1757, March 17.
[21] Dinwiddie Papers, vol. ii, p. 720.

that Part of the Country I must again refer it to Colo. Washington, and what he does will meet with my Approbation, but at the same Time consider if it will not be disagreeable to L'd Loudoun to leave the front'rs if the different Forts are not commanded by good Officers, and L'd Loudoun is not yet come to his Winter Q'rs, but is now at F't Edward, w'ch will be a long Journey. However, as above, I leave it to Colo. Washington. I'm glad to hear Cox and Lane got safe in to Capt. McKenzie's Fort, and their Skirmish shows the Necessity of Detachments from all the Forts to be out in Ranging Parties, w'ch at times may probably find some of the Enemy in their Lurking Places; and this Duty I have frequently recommended and ordered, and I'm Convinced it wou'd prove of essential Service. I shall be glad to hear of Capt. McKenzie's Return, as it will be attended with Danger. Yo. do not mention the No. that March'd with him. As the Man-of-War I expected to accommodate me home is not yet arrived, it makes my Departure very uncertain. I wish yo. Health, and I rem.,

S'r Y'r H'ble Serv't.

APPENDIX I

PIONEER FORTS, STOCKADES, AND BLOCK-HOUSES ON THE VIRGINIA FRONTIER DURING THE PERIOD OF THE FRENCH AND INDIAN WAR.

The following list of forts[1] on the Virginia Frontier, for the period of the French and Indian War, is arranged alphabetically. Brief statements are made as to the location, history, and citations to original sources of information, or to authorities having had access thereto, concerning each fort, stockade, and block-house mentioned.

(1) FORT ASHBY[2]

Fort Ashby was a stockade on the east bank of Patterson's Creek, twelve miles from the " Fort at Cockes's " on the same stream. It was erected in 1755 by Lieutenant John Bacon under orders from Colonel Washington, on the site of the present village of Alaska, Mineral County, West Virginia. It had a garrison of sixty men. Washington wrote to Governor Dinwiddie from Alexandria, January 14, 1756, with reference to Fort Ashby:

I have already built two forts on Patterson's Creek, (which have engaged the chief part on the inhabitants to return to their

---

[1] References to frontier defense are as follows: Ford, Writings of Washington, vol. i, pp. 236, 256, 261, 262, 292-293, 295-296, 325, 347, 371-373; Lieutenant Colonel Adam Stephens, letter to Washington, from Fort Cumberland, August 1, 1756, Hamilton, vol. i, pp. 328-330; William Fairfax to Washington, from Belvoir, May 13, 1756 (ibid., p. 257); Appendix II, No. 8.

[2] Wills De Haas, History of the Early Settlement and Indian Wars of Virginia, p. 204; Kercheval, History of the Valley, ed. of 1833, p. 126; Washington's Journal over the Mountains, 1747-1748, Toner, ed.; Journal of Captain Charles Lewis, printed in the Collections of the Virginia Historical Society, vol. xi, p. 216, n. s.; Dinwiddie Papers, vol. ii, p. 239; Sparks, Writings of Washington, vol. ii, pp. 11, 125, 163, 167; Hamilton, Letters to Washington, vol. i, pp. 157, 162, 220, 267, 303, 321, 330; V. A. Lewis, First Biennial Report of Archives and History of West Virginia, p. 207; Ford, Writings of Washington, vol. i, pp. 274, 275, 298, 372.

plantations:) and have now ordered Captain Waggener with sixty men to build and garrison two others, (at places I have pointed out high up on the South Branch,) which will be a means of securing near an hundred miles of our frontiers, exclusive of the command at Fort Dinwiddie, on Jackson's River.

On December 27, 1755, Captain Lewis, of Fredericksburg, assumed command at this fort in which he found a garrison of twenty-one men. The next spring, May 23, 1756, Colonel Washington issued orders to Lieutenant-Colonel Adam Stephen to have "the forts of Ashby, Cockes, etc., plentifully furnished" from Fort Cumberland, Maryland, twenty-five miles away. In August of that year, Lieutenant Robert Rutherford, with a company of rangers, was defeated here by the Indians. Captain John Ashby in 1756 made a remarkable escape from the Indians, reaching this fort in safety.

(2) WALLACE AUSTIN'S FORT [3]

The record we have of Austin's Fort is rather fragmentary. The fort stood on Bull Pasture River, in present Pocahontas or Greenbrier County, West Virginia. William Preston was engaged in building it early in April, 1757, in pursuance of orders of February 26, 1757. It was eighty feet square and its walls were the "best of the kind in the country." Preston had called together the people in the Bull Pasture region to meet him at Wallace Austin's "to consult on a proper place to build a fort for their Defense." Nine of the men who met together there voted for the location of the fort on the Bull Pasture River. Local preferences thus sometimes determined the location of the less important forts. Preston paid the "15 good Hands" a shilling a day for their work. The fort having been begun March 8, he hoped to complete it in "six or seven days," but bad weather retarded his progress and the inhabitants round about gave little of the aid promised. Besides, as he reported, "I could not get one man to join the work until I agreed to see him Paid." The total cost Preston reckoned at about £15.

---

[3] Preston to Lewis, April 4, 1757, Draper, MSS., Preston Papers, 1QQ152.

(3) FORT BRACKENRIDGE [4]

Fort Brackenridge was situated on Jackson's River, in Greenbrier County, West Virginia, sixteen miles from Dickinson's Fort on the same stream. Its garrison was forty men. Washington, Colonel Buchanan, and others visited it in the fall of 1756.

(4) FORT BUTTERMILK [5]

Fort Buttermilk was a stockade. It was situated on the South Branch of the Potomac, about three miles above the present site of Moorfield, in Hardy County, West Virginia. It was erected by Captain Thomas Waggoner under orders from Colonel Washington in 1756. Eighteen men from this fort joined the garrison from Fort Pleasant in the desperate "Battle of the Trough" on the South Branch in 1756. Washington's memorandum book, as given in Ford's Writings of Washington (volume i, page 274), states that on May 14, 1756 the garrison "At Waggener's uppr. F." was fifty men from Culpeper. On May 16, 1757, Governor Dinwiddie ordered Washington to station seventy men under Captain Thomas Waggoner at this fort. For this reason some writers refer to the place as "Fort Waggoner."

(5) FORT CAPON [6]

Fort Capon was a small stockade defense which stood at the "Forks of Capon" in the Great Cacapon Valley, in present Hampshire County, West Virginia. The men who garrisoned it cultivated the fertile fields of low ground about four miles from the fort. In 1757 or 1758, two of them, one named Bowers, the other York, returning from their work, were waylaid by seven Indians. Bowers was killed

---

[4] Ford, Writings of Washington, vol. i, p. 372; Virginia Magazine of History and Biography, vol. xv, pp. 247-251; Hamilton, vol. ii, p. 306.

[5] Ford, Writings of Washington, Washington to Dinwiddie, January 14, 1756, vol. i, p. 221; Hamilton, vol. ii, pp. 72, 96; see Fort Ashby above.

[6] Kercheval, History of the Valley, ed. of 1833, p. 126; Lewis, p. 208.

and scalped but his companion finally succeeded in gaining the fort.

(6) FORT CHISWELL [7]

Fort Chiswell was constructed in 1758 at the meeting point of the Richmond and Valley of Virginia trails, at "the forks of the road." It was built as a protection against the Cherokees. Its location was on a portage between the Holston and the New Rivers, just west of the eighty-first meridian.

(7) FORT CHRISTY [8]

Fort Christy was located on Jackson's River, fifteen miles from Fort Dinwiddie on the same stream, and eighteen miles from Trout Rock, farther up the river. Its garrison was forty men.

(8)   FORT COX [9]

Fort Cox was a stockade situated, according to Vergil A. Lewis, on the lower point of land on the Potomac at the mouth of the Little Cacapon River. Here, on April 25, 1750, George Washington, then eighteen years of age, surveyed a tract of two hundred forty acres for his "Friend Cox." Ford's Writings of Washington, volume i, page 311, says: "This Fort was on Patterson's Creek, twenty-five miles from Fort Cumberland." It is shown on Washington's map of the Upper Potomac (1756); also, on Thomas Hutchins' Topographical Map of Virginia and Pennsylvania, published in London, 1778, by order of Parliament. Colonel Washington, on May 23, 1756, gave orders to Lieutenant-Colonel Adam Stephen to have Fort Cox furnished supplies from Fort Cumberland, Maryland; and on May 5, 1756, Washington wrote John Robinson, Speaker of the House of Burgesses, recommending that Fort Cox be made the depot of

[7] L. P. Summers, History of Southwest Virginia; Semple, American History and Its Geographic Condition; Journals, 1761-1765, pp. 211, 213, 244.

[8] Ford, Writings of Washington, vol. i, p. 372.

[9] Hamilton, vol. i, p. 162; vol. ii, p. 277; Ford, Writings of Washington, vol. i, pp. 272, 274, 311, 372.

supplies for the upper Potomac defenses. Washington, when on his journey to the Ohio in 1770, was on the spot where Fort Cox had stood, but it had disappeared. Washington, who spelled the name "Cocke's," considered this fort an important defense, and he included it in his plan of forts sumbitted in 1756.

(9) CRAIG'S CREEK FORT [10]

Very little is known of Craig's Creek Fort. Andrew Lewis wrote to Governor Dinwiddie in June, 1756, that he had "Ordered Captain Dunlap with a Company to a Fort at the mouth of Craig's Creek, and the Bedford Militia I hope will protect the Roanoke." In Washington's plan of forts drawn up in the fall of 1756, he lists the Craik's (Craigs) Creek fort as "Not built."

(10) COLONEL CRISSOP'S FORT [11]

Colonel Crissop's Fort stood upon Colonel Thomas Cresop's farm, "Shipton," a few miles above the North and South Branches of the Potomac. Captain Thomas Cocke's Journal records, October 5, 1755, that, ". . . the french & Indians had killed Several Families and Besieged Col¹ Crissops Fort."

(11) FORT CUMBERLAND [12]

Fort Cumberland (the location being sometimes referred to as Will's Creek), where present Cumberland, Maryland, stands, was an important point. The Ohio Land Company built a warehouse there as early as 1750. The location lay directly across the path westward from Virginia, Maryland, and even southern Pennsylvania, to the "forks of the Ohio." Braddock's route led by it.

---

[10] Draper, MSS., Preston Papers, 1QQ131-133.
[11] Hamilton, vol. i, p. 117; vol. ii, p. 57.
[12] Ford, Writings of Washington, vol. i, p. 364; Blair, Report on Colonies, section on Maryland, 1756, p. 9 (Loudoun Papers, Blair file); see Appendix II, No. 8.

This fort was the occasion of numerous disputes between Maryland and Virginia. The fort stood on Maryland territory, yet it was directly on the way from tidewater Virginia to Fort Duquesne and was of great strategic importance to Virginia. There were constant differences between these two colonies as to how strongly guarded this place should be, and who should furnish the garrison. Usually, Maryland furnished half of it and Virginia the other half.

At Fort Cumberland a council of war was held on October 30, 1756, " in pursuance of an Order received from Colonel George Washington, agreeable to an order from Governor Dinwiddie to consult whether it is most for the advantage of His Majesty's Service, to keep or demolish Fort Cumberland.[13]

PRESENT
Lieut. Colo: Adam Stephen, President.
Members:

Capt. Wm. Bronaugh	Capt. Hen. Woodward
Capt. Robt. Spotswood	Capt. Chas. Lewis
Capt. Wm. Peachy	Lt. Peter Steenberger
Lt. Austin Brockenborough	Lt. James Baker
Lt. Mordecai Buckner	Ens. Wm. Dangerfield
Ensn. Edwd. Hubbard	Ens. Nathl. Thompson
Ens. Charles Smith	Ens. Jno. Lawson "
Ens. Griffin Pert	

It was determined to continue the fort, although Washington considered it " a place very useless in itself, and expensive to the country, containing over 150 men solely employed in guarding the stores, which could be better defended at any other place."

Washington, in 1756, submitted a plan for twenty-two forts to guard the frontier. " It will be seen," he says, that " Fort Cumberland is not mentioned in this plan. If we act only on the defensive (a system on which this plan is founded) I think it employs a large garrison to very little advantage to Virginia. If we act offensively, it may be of

---

[13] Washington could not be present, as he was visiting the forts along the southern frontier (Ford, Writings of Washington, vol. i, pp. 364-368).

infinite use, if properly fortified, and the Garrison at Cockes's will then only consist of about 50 or 60, as the rest may be removed to Fort Cumberland." [14]

Washington wrote to Dinwiddie from Alexandria, January 14, 1756, that the Fort Cumberland "situation, which is extremely bad, will ever be an eyesore to this colony. . . ." [15]

Lord Loudoun wrote from Albany on September 22, 1756: "I do hope and trust that the Government of Virginia will not suffer the post of Fort Cumberland to be wrested from them." Dinwiddie instructed Washington to maintain the fort if possible. [16]

(12) FORT DEFIANCE [17]

Fort Defiance was situated on the South Branch of the Potomac, twenty miles from Fort Pleasant on the same branch. Its allotted garrison was sixty men.

(13) FORT DICKINSON [18]

Fort Dickinson stood on the Cow Pasture River, eighteen miles from Craig's Creek, a branch of the James River, about four miles below present Millsborough, Virginia. It had a garrison of two hundred and fifty men. Major Lewis wrote to William Preston, August 27, 1757, from Dickinson's Fort, that the governor had given him permission "to dispose of your and Dickinson's companys as I think best for the protection of the poor inhabitants." And Washington, from Winchester, wrote about Fort Dickinson to Dinwiddie, November 9, 1756, in the same letter in which he referred to Fort Ashby.

---

[14] Ibid., p. 373.
[15] Ibid., p. 221.
[16] Ibid., p. 371.
[17] Ibid., p. 372.
[18] Ibid., pp. 372, 376; Virginia Magazine of History and Biography, vol. xv, pp. 247-251; Draper, MSS., Preston Papers, 1QQ158; Journals, 1756-1758, p. 462; Hamilton, vol. i, pp. 109, 285, vol. ii, pp. 53, 72.

(14)   FORT DINWIDDIE [19]

Fort Dinwiddie (known also as Warwick's Fort, Hog's Fort, and Byrd's Fort), an important defense, stood in Augusta County, in what is now Bath County, Virginia, on the Irwin place on Jackson's River, fourteen miles from Brackenridge's fort on the same stream. Its garrison, maintained from 1754 to 1789, varied from sixty to one hundred men. Washington wrote to Captain Hog of the Virginia Regiment, July 21, 1756:

As the Assembly has voted a chain of Forts to be built on the Frontier, the Governor has ordered out the Militia of Augusta to assist you in erecting them . . . to the Southward of Fort Dinwiddie, extending the Line towards Mayo River as directed by the Assembly.

He was to make use of his own company of men and of the militia he might raise, " except about 30 private wh. you are to leave under the Command of Lt. Bullett, at Fort Dinwiddie. . . ." Fort Dinwiddie was visited by Washington, Colonel Buchanan, and party in the fall of 1756. Washington had previously visited it on September 24, 1755, and he had always considered it a strong position. Captain Hog wrote to Washington from Fort Dinwiddie, September 23, 1755: " As to provisions there is not any in the fort in case it Should be Besieged, there is no Salt to Cure any, or even to Season the fresh Meat till it comes up from Fredericksburg. Maj'r Lewis has Engaged about 24 days provisions, but he has no money to Leave with me to purchase more, neither should I incline to take the trouble for a Sett of men who repay such Services with scandalous reflections."

(15)   FORT AT DRAPER'S MEADOWS [20]

Dinwiddie wrote to Colonel Clement Read on September 8, 1756: " Give Stallicker 100 (£) to qualify him to take

---

[19] Hamilton, vol. i, pp. 92-94, 105, 106-108, 109, 137-138, 151, 261, 286-287; vol. ii, pp. 15, 185, 200-201; Journals, 1761-1765, p. 254; Dinwiddie Papers, vol. ii, pp. 241, 316, 460; Ford, Writings of Washington, vol. i, p. 188.

[20] Dinwiddie Papers, vol. ii, p. 503.

his Company and build a little Stockade Fort at Draper's Meadows, and take his receipt for it."

(16) Dunlap's Fort [21]

Our information is very meager regarding this fort, which is also spelled Fort Dunlop. Captain Preston wrote to Major Lewis, October 29, 1757, that he had " an order of Court to be at Dunlaps Fort this Week to take a list of the Tithables." Two Cartwell children, he added, were taken from this fort "last Thursday." Other references in the Lewis-Preston correspondence indicate that one must pass Dunlap's Fort on the way to Fort Young on Jackson River. The Journals of the House of Burgesses record the reading of a " Petition of John Dickenson, setting forth that he went out Captain of a Company of Volunteers of Augusta County, in Pursuit of the Indians who have of late infested those Parts, in October last . . . that he may be allowed for a Quantity of Provisions laid in at Fort Dunlop."

(17) Fort Du Quesne, Later Fort Pitt [22]

The Ohio Company had a trading post at the " forks of the Ohio " as early as 1750. Captain Trent was sent out in 1753 to fortify the place. He had, however, not completed his defenses before the French from Venango north of him swooped down in overwhelming numbers and compelled him to evacuate the place. They finished the fortifications he had begun and named it Fort Du Quesne, in honor of the governor-general of Canada. The French held this important point until the time of General Forbes' expedition against it in 1758, when the French and Indians evacuated and burned it upon the approach of the English. The Eng-

[21] Draper, MSS., Preston Papers, 1QQ163; Journals, 1761-1765, p. 215.

[22] Ford, Writings of Washington, vol. ii, pp. 17, 87, 90, 114, 116, 120, 192; vol. vii, pp. 30, 218, vol. ix, pp. 8, 455; Dinwiddie Papers, vol. i, pp. 113, 185, 487, and passim, vol. ii, pp. 119, 629, 676; Journals, 1752-1755, p. 291; 1756-1758, pp. 351, 366; Hamilton, vol. i, p. 70.

lish erected a stronghold there and renamed it Fort Pitt, out of gratitude to the great minister who had helped so directly to make their success possible. The city of Pittsburgh has grown up at this strategic point.

(18) FORT EDWARDS [23]

Fort Edwards was a stockade defense situated on or near the site of the present village of Capon Bridge, on Capon River, in present Hampshire County, West Virginia. From Fort Edwards, on April 18, 1756, Captain John Mercer, with one hundred men [24] of Washington's Regiment, went in pursuit of a body of thirty or forty Frenchmen and Shawnese Indians known to be in the vicinity. The result was an ambuscade in which Captain Mercer and all but six of his men were killed and scalped. Washington, who was then in Winchester, upon hearing of Mercer's fate, wrote Lord Fairfax, county-lieutenant of Frederick County, urging him to order out militia for the defense of the border settlements. He said to Fairfax, April 19, 1756: "Unless I can throw some ammunition into Edwards's Fort to night, the remainder of our party, and the inhabitants that are there, will more than probably fall a sacrifice to the Indians. . . ." But to rely upon the militia of Frederick County, Washington termed "an unhappy reliance." [25]

(19) ENOCH'S FORT [26]

While Washington's list of frontier defenses drawn up in the fall of 1756, lists this fort as "Enochs, not built," he considered the place important, and in his apportionment of troops for the string of forts he allotted it 75 men. In his memorandum book for 1756, Washington lists "35 (men from) Louisa At Enochs's." The location of the place was

---

[23] Hamilton, vol. i, pp. 223, 243, 247, vol. ii, pp. 72, 96, 321; Lewis, pp. 208-209.
[24] Kercheval (ed. of 1833), p. 102, says forty men were under Captain Mercer.
[25] Ford, Writings of Washington, vol. i, p. 248.
[26] Ibid., p. 372.

on the Cacapehon fifteen miles from Fort Maidstone on the Potomac, and forty-five miles from Fort Loudoun at Winchester.

(20) FORT EVANS [27]

Fort Evans was a stockade situated two miles south of Martinsburg, at the head of what is called Big Spring, in Berkeley County, West Virginia. It was begun by John Evans, in the fall of 1755, but not completed until the spring of the following year. Scarcely was it completed when, in 1756, the Indians made an incursion into the vicinity, and the people, among them the founders of Martinsburg, found refuge in this fort. The Indians then burned the house of John Evans's brother. The garrison left the fort to bury a man by the name of Kelly, whom the Indians had killed, and in their absence the fort was attacked. The heroic conduct of Mrs. Evans, wife of the builder of the fort, saved it from capture and the women and children within from massacre.

(21) FARLEY'S FORT [28]

Thomas Farley from Albemarle County, Virginia, in 1754, obtained a tract of land near Crump's Bottom, in the southern part of what is now Summers County, West Virginia, and erected a fort on the south bank of the New River, near what is known as "Warford." This fort was farther west than either McNeil's Fort or Fort William, the later on the Catawba branch of the James.

(22) FORT FAUQUIER [29]

From here, while commanding a company at the place, John Buchanan and Lieutenant Joseph McDowell furnished flour and beef to sundry individuals. Their "account against the country" (1758-1759) is given in the Preston Papers.

---

[27] Kercheval (ed. of 1833), pp. 94-95; F. V. Aler, History of Martinsburg and Berkeley County, p. 39; Lewis, p. 209.

[28] J. M. Callahan, Semi-Centennial History of West Virginia, p. 19; D. E. Johnston, A History of the Middle New River Settlements, p. 14.

[29] Draper, MSS., Preston Papers, 2QQ 3, 5, 9, 14, 15, 18.

(23) FORT FREDERIC [30]

In May, 1756, Governor Sharpe and his assembly had
come to temporary agreement and the assembly had voted
£40,000 for His Majesty's service, of which sum £11,000 was
to be appropriated to the building of a fort on the frontier,
but not beyond North Mountain. The fort constructed was
called Fort Frederic, and was situated on the north side of
the river at the point where the seventy-eighth meridian
crosses the Potomac River. Washington says: [31] " It was
a work of considerable magnitude, situated on an eminence
about 500 yds. from the Potomac River, of a quadrangular
form, and constructed of durable materials."

(24) FORT FREDERICK [32]

Fort Frederick stood on the New River, at or near, the
vicinity of Ingles' Ferry, and not on the Roanoke as Taylor
and Withers would have it, says Dr. Lyman C. Draper. [33]
Major Andrew Lewis' men rendezvoused there for the Big
Sandy River (or Sandy Creek) expedition in the early part
of 1756. There were about three hundred and forty-six men
in the army including one hundred and thirty Cherokees.

(25) FORT FURMAN [34]

This stockade was situated on the South Branch of the
Potomac, about one mile above Hanging Rock, and three
miles north of what is now Romney, Hampshire County,
West Virginia. It was built at the beginning of the French
and Indian War by William Furman who, with Nimrod

---

[30] Ford, Writings of Washington, vol. i, p. 290; J. V. L. Mc-
Mahon, History of Maryland, vol. i, p. 305.

[31] Ford, Writings of Washington, vol. i, p. 290.

[32] Journals, 1756-1758, pp. 369, 380, 395, 426; 1761-1765, p. 297;
Draper, MSS., Preston Papers, 1QQ94-123; ibid., Frontier Wars
MSS., vol. iv, pp. 1-3; Campbell, pp. 489-490.

[33] Draper, MSS., 1U1-8.

[34] Kercheval (ed. of 1833), pp. 128-131; De Haas, p. 212; J. L.
Peyton, History of Augusta County, pp. 117-118; Lewis, p. 210.

Ashby, was killed by a band of Delaware Indians on Jersey [35] Mountain in 1764. Many atrocities occurred in this vicinity.

(26) CAPTAIN GALLOWAY'S FORT [36]

Captain Galloway's Fort was situated on Smith's River, fifteen miles from Captain Harris' Fort on the Mayo River, and had a garrison of twenty men.

(27) FORT GEORGE [37]

Fort George (sometimes erroneously referred to as Fort Prince George) was an important fort which stood on the Roanoke near where Salem, Virginia, now stands. This stronghold was not far from Fort Lewis, and there is some justification for believing that the two places were identical. From this place Captain William Preston and his company set out on the Sandy Creek expedition against the Shawnee Indians on the Ohio, February 9, 1756. Captain Preston was later in command of this fort for a time. Fort George is mentioned frequently in the Preston Papers, the statements informing us as to the work at the fort, the value of services of that day, and the prices of commodities. These are some of the entries: John Carlisle, August 12, 1757, hands a receipt to William Preston for 17s. 3d. for six and one-half day's work at Fort George (Preston Papers, 6QQ17); John Estill's receipt to William Preston, August 12, 1757, for 7s. for seven days' work at Fort George (Preston Papers, 6QQ18); receipts likewise in 1757 and 1758 from John Folley, Joseph Marlin, Samuel Montaney, John Prior, John Smith, William Stewart, Abraham Bailey, Joseph Bell, John Johnston, Edward Hinds, John Miller, John Fite, Robert Knox, Philip Phagen, John Hamilton, James McKnight,

---

[35] So named from its being first settled by people from New Jersey.

[36] Ford, Writings of Washington, vol. i, p. 372.

[37] Draper, MSS., Preston Papers; Johnston, p. 23; Journals, 1761-1765, p. 236. This fort is not to be confused with Fort George on the east bank of the South Branch of the Potomac or with Fort George that stood at Old Point Comfort.

Thomas Mullen, James Burnsides, Hugh Bodkin, Josiah Cummings, John Davies, John Jackson, Sr., John Miller, William Sharpe, William Black, John McCreery, Richard Mihills (Preston Papers, 6QQ16-137); on July 3, 1758, John Vance gave his receipt to William Preston for £2 14s. 6d. for carrying flour from Staunton to the Calf Pasture and to Fort George (Preston Papers, 6QQ54); on October 5, 1757, John Davies received from William Preston £2 13s. 4d. for forty days' service as a corporal at Fort George prior to May 1, 1757 (Preston Papers, 6QQ88); on October 11, 1757, George Campbell gave William Preston a receipt for 5s. 6d. for a spade used in building Fort George (Preston Papers, 6QQ22). Another entry (in 1758) is Richard Mihills' receipt to William Preston for 7s. 6d. for salting beef at Fort George in November, 1758 (Preston Papers, 6QQ130). These are only scraps of information, but they are valuable. We should be fortunate to be able to secure even so fragmentary a record for the other forts of our list.

The Journals of the House of Burgesses contain a reference to Fort George, the minutes referring to "A Petition of Robert Breckenridge, setting forth that he commanded a Committee of Militia of Augusta County, which was stationed at Fort George for Part of the Month of December, all of January, and to the 22d day of February, 1759."

(28) FORT GEORGE [38]

Fort George was a small stockade fort located on the east bank of the South Branch of the Potomac nearly opposite the present town of Petersburg, in Grant County, West Virginia. It was built about the year 1754, presumably by Job Welton and his brothers. In 1756, one of the brothers, a man named De Lay, and two others who had left the fort to mow a meadow nearby, were killed and scalped. Job Welton, badly wounded, escaped to the fort. Soon after, a man by the name of Powers was killed nearby, and it was in this vicinity that eight (Kercheval, p. 115, says seven) Indians attacked

---

[38] Lewis, p. 210; Journals, 1758-1761, p. 21.

the cabin of Samuel Bingaman, who made a heroic defense. He killed six of them, the seventh saving himself by flight.

(29) Fort Harness [39]

Fort Harness was eighty-one miles west of Fort Loudoun and had a garrison varying from seventeen to fifty men. Washington reported in his memorandum book on May 14, 1756, that it was garrisoned then by fifty men from Stafford. On the 17th of May, following, twenty-five men from Orange County were substituted for the Stafford contingent at the fort. A council of war, presided over by Captain Thomas Waggoner, was held there on August 10, 1756, to consider the disposition of troops "in the most eligible manner for the protection of the Inhabitants above yᵉ Trough . . . as the Militia stationed upon the Branch are determined to leave their Stations directly." The following members of the council were present: Captain Thomas Waggoner, President, Captains Thomas Cocke, Robert Spotswood, William Bronaugh, David Bell, Lieutenants Walter Stewart, John King, Mordecai Buckner, and Ensigns John Dean, Jethro Sumner, and Charles Smith. John Lomax also signed the findings of the council.

(30) Fort at Matthew Harper's [40]

This defense was situated on the Bull Pasture River, in the northern part of present Highland County, Virginia, twenty miles from Trout Rock and eighteen miles from Captain Miller's Fort. Its garrison was fifty men.

(31) Captain Harris' Fort [41]

Captain Harris' Fort was located on Mayo River, and in Washington's plan for the forts drawn in 1756 it occupied

[39] Hamilton, vol. i, pp. 331-332, vol. ii, p. 96; Ford, Writings of Washington, vol. i, pp. 274-275.
[40] Virginia Magazine of History and Biography, vol. xv, pp. 247-251; Hamilton, vol. i, pp. 305-306.
[41] Ford, Writings of Washington, vol. i, p. 372.

the most southern position in the line. Washington suggested a garrison of twenty men each for Terry's, Galloway's, and Harris' forts.

(32) HICKEY'S FORT [42]

The fragmentary information about this defense tells us only that the traveller passed Hickey's Fort, probably a block-house, on the way to the Mayo Fort.

(33) FORT HEDGES [43]

Fort Hedges was a small stockade on the west side of Back Creek on the road now leading from Martinsburg to Berkeley Springs, Berkeley County, West Virginia. This vicinity was the scene of many Indian atrocities.

(34) CAPTAIN HOG'S FORT [44]

Captain Hog's Fort was situated on the Roanoke River, twenty-six miles from Captain Terry's Fort and was allotted a garrison of one hundred and fifty men.

(35) FORT HOPEWELL [45]

Fort Hopewell was situated on the South Branch of the Potomac, but the exact location is not definitely known. On April 24, 1754, Colonel Washington enclosed to Governor Dinwiddie a letter which, he says, "was just sent to me from Fort Hopewell, on the South Branch. They have had an engagement there, with the French and Indians, the particulars of which you will see by the enclosed. Captain Waggoner, with a party of his men, joined them next day and went in pursuit of the enemy, but could not come up with them." The name of the fort may have been sug-

---

[42] L. P. Summers, History of Southwest Virginia, p. 66.
[43] Kercheval (ed. of 1833), p. 115; De Haas, p. 204; Lewis, p. 210.
[44] Ford, Writings of Washington, vol. i, p. 372; Hamilton, vol. i, p. 94. This fort is not to be confused with Hog's Fort (Fort Dinwiddie), above, p. 118.
[45] Ford Writings of Washington, vol. i, p. 254; Lewis, pp. 210-211.

gested, thinks Vergil A. Lewis, by that of the British sloop, "Hopewell," visiting the waters of Virginia at that time.

(36) KELLER'S FORT [46]

Keller's Fort is mentioned by De Haas as being about fifteen miles from Powell's Fort. Both were some ten miles from the present Woodstock, Virginia.

(37) KIRKENDALL'S FORT [47]

The structure seem to have been only a temporary defense, and probably only a block-house at that, as it is referred to but once by Washington. His memorandum book for May 17, 1756, states that on that date there were forty-five men from Fairfax stationed at the place. Its exact location is not known.

(38) FORT LEWIS [48]

Our records for this fort, probably located near Salem, Virginia, are extremely fragmentary. The Preston Papers contain many references to Fort Lewis, chiefly receipts and acknowledgments for money, services, and provisions. The detached entries, all acknowledgments held by Preston, and valuable chiefly for their personal references, run, for example: Captain William Preston's receipt from Robert Hall, August 4, 1757, for 27s. for twenty-seven days' service at Fort Lewis (6QQ68); James Shaw's receipt to Captain William Preston, August 11, 1757, for £1 as pay for patrolling at Fort Lewis; also 14s. 6d. for salt and the use of a horse for two days (6QQ68); William Stewart's receipt to William Preston, August 12, 1757, for 10s. for carrying provisions to Fort Lewis (6QQ24); James Miller's receipt to Captain William Preston, August 27, 1757, for £1 16s. for thirty-six days' service at Fort Lewis (6QQ69); the receipt

---

[46] De Haas, p. 205.
[47] Ford, Writings of Washington, vol. i, p. 275.
[48] Draper, MSS., Preston Papers, passim; Journals, 1761-1765, pp. x, xvii, 33; there were at least 200 men in the fort in 1761 (Journals, 1758-1761, p. 278).

is witnessed by Thomas Lloyd and signed by a mark, as are many of the receipts in the Preston Papers. Michael Willgong's receipt to William Preston, September 20, 1757, for 14s. 4d. for provisions delivered at Fort Lewis. This statement is witnessed by Loftus Pullin (6QQ34); Philip Phagen's receipt to William Preston, September 22, 1757, for 6s. for six days' work at Fort Lewis (6QQ20); James Knox's receipt to William Preston, September 25, 1757, for 16s. 6d. for provisions delivered to Sergeant Hugart at Fort Lewis (6QQ33); William Black's receipt to William Preston, October 5, 1757, for 34s. for pay as a soldier at Fort Lewis (6QQ70); John Davies' receipt to William Preston, October 5, 1757, £3 13s. 4d. for fifty-five days' pay as a corporal at Fort Lewis (6QQ69); Charles Gilham's receipt to William Preston, October 5, 1757, for 19s. 6d. in payment for work at Fort Lewis (6QQ35); John Jordan's receipt to William Preston, October 12, 1757, for £1 13s. for thirty-three days' service as a soldier at Fort Lewis (6QQ91); William Wilson's receipt to William Preston, October 12, 1757, for 2s. for four turnips delivered at Fort Lewis (6QQ37); also, same to same, October 12, 1757, £2 2s. for forty-two days' service as a soldier at Fort Lewis (6QQ70); John Jackson, Sr.'s receipt to William Preston, October 13, 1757, for £4 5s. for eighty-five days' service as a soldier in his company prior to May 1, 1757 (6QQ94); George Wilson's receipt to William Preston, October 13, 1757, for £2 17s. 2d. for provisions delivered to Sergeant Hugart at Fort Lewis (6QQ38); Samuel Bright's receipt to William Preston (1757), for £1 10s. for thirty days' service as a soldier at Fort Lewis. The transaction is witnessed by Adam Jordan (6QQ72); Thomas Hugart's receipt to William Preston (1757), for £3 18s. 8d. for fifty-nine days' pay as a sergeant at Fort Lewis prior to May 1, 1757 (6QQ72).

Colonel Stephen, in command of the Virginia regiment raised in the spring of 1761 to act in cooperation with the troops of North Carolina under Colonel Grant, maintained his force first at Big Island in the Cherokee country, then at " Stalnaker's." Here he remained until he was able to advise Governor Fauquier that articles of peace had been signed between Governor Bull and the chiefs of the Cherokee nation, when he was ordered to march to Fort Lewis, in the county of Augusta, and disband his regiment, which he did May 1, 1763.

(39) FORT ON LONG ISLAND [49]

Colonel William Byrd's headquarters, during his campaign against the Cherokee "Over Hill" towns in 1760, was a fort at the Long Island on the upper Holston in East Tennessee.

(40) LOONEY'S FORT [50]

Looney's Fort was situated at the mouth of Looney's Creek, at Looney's Ferry, on the James River, where, according to the Jefferson and Fry Map of 1751, "The Great Road from the Yadkin River thro Virginia to Philadelphia distance 435 Miles," crossed the river. Andrew Lewis wrote to Governor Dinwiddie in June, 1756, that he had "Ordered ten men to Looney's Fort on James River." In the summer of 1761, a party of about sixty Shawnese Indians penetrated the settlements on the James River, avoided this fort, and killed and plundered the people in the vicinity of Purgatory Mountain and Purgatory Creek.

(41) FORT LOUDOUN [51]

Fort Loudoun was a strong fort built by Colonel Washington in 1756. It stood near the present town of Winchester, Virginia, which in those days was sometimes known as Frederick Town. This fort had a long and honorable his-

---

[49] Semple, p. 61; Draper, MSS., Virginia Papers, 3ZZ35; Hamilton, vol. i, p. 94.

[50] Ibid., Preston Papers, 1QQ131-133; A. S. Withers, Chronicles of Border Warfare, p. 67.

[51] Dinwiddie Papers, vol. ii, pp. 525, 559, 572, 616; Ford, Writings of Washington, vol. i, pp. 285, 433; vol. ii, pp. 8, 29; Hening, vol. vii, pp. 33, 357, 358; Campbell, pp. 493, 494; Kercheval, ed. of 1833, p. 91; Mrs. Danske Dandridge, Historic Shepherdstown, p. 32; Hamilton, vol. i, p. 202; vol. ii, pp. 21, 53, 61, 94, 95; vol. iii, p. 197; the act of assembly authorizing this fort, March 12, 1756, is given in Hamilton, vol. i, p. 202.

tory. It commanded the lower Shenandoah Valley and lay in the path of the Indian trails and the "Philadelphia Waggon Road" running north and south through Virginia. It was important as a base of supplies for the western Virginia Frontier, particularly for the then large territory of Federick County. It was here that Washington made his headquarters during the critical years on the Virginia Frontier. "Winchester," Washington said in 1756, "is the center, as it were, of all the forts. . . . It also lies in a vale of land that has suffered more than any other from the incursions of the enemy." Charles Campbell, the historian, says, "Fort Loudoun was erected at Winchester, the key of that region, under his (Washington's) superintendence. It was a square with four bastions; the batteries mounted twenty-four guns; a well was sunk, mostly through a bed of limestone; the barracks were sufficient for four hundred and fifty men. Vestiges of this fortification still remain. Winchester, after the erection of Fort Loudoun, increased rapidly, owing to its being the rendezvous of the Virginia troops; in 1759 it contained two hundred houses."

(42) FORT LOUDOUN ON THE HOLSTON [52]

This fort (often known and referred to as "Fort at Choto," spelled also Choté, Chote, Chotte) was built in 1756 by Andrew Lewis of Virginia, under orders from Governor Dinwiddie, on the Holston (Tennessee River), one hundred and fifty miles beyond the western settlements of North Carolina, and thirty miles southwest of present Knoxville, Tennessee. "The Plan and Profile of Fort Loudoun Latitude 36° 7^m Projected by William D. Brahm his Majestys Surveyor Genl in Georgia," may be seen in its original drawing among the Loudoun Papers under date of February 19, 1757, in the Huntington Library. Many early surveyors were under error in computing locations. The site of Fort

---

[52] Hening, vol. vii, p. 62; Dinwiddie Papers, vol. i, pp. 267, 273; vol. ii, pp. 202, 267, 390-391, 394, 444; Loudoun Papers, Dinwiddie file, 1756, August 28; ibid., Lewis file, 1756, July 23; Journals, 1756-1758, p. 404, 1758-1761, pp. xiv, 263n.

Loudoun is marked by the town of Loudon, county seat of Loudon county, Tennessee, which lies south of the thirty-sixth parallel.

This famous fort stood in the so-called Upper Cherokee Country and was erected at a cost of £7,000; of this amount the king contributed £1,000, and the provinces the remainder. Dinwiddie's letter of instruction to Major Andrew Lewis bears the date of April 24, 1756, and is given in the Dinwiddie Papers, vol. ii, pp. 390-301. "As it is determin'd to assist the Cherokees in build'g a Fort to defend y'r Women & Children from the Insults of the French w'n they go to War in assist'g y'r Bro's, the English, You are accordingly appointed to overseer the build'g of the s'd Fort, I therefore empower you to enlist 60 Men for the s'd Service, and I order You to be careful in enlist'g many Tradesmen y't can use the Saw and Ax for the Construct'n of the s'd Fort, and You are to give them such Pay as You may think proper, tak'g great Care to be as frugal as possible." He was to be provided with " proper Tools, w'h 10,000 lbs. Flour " and with " 700 £ to purchase 100 head of Beeves to drive along with You. . . ."

Major Lewis reported to Dinwiddie, July 23, 1756, in his own peculiar style (a contemporary copy is in the Lewis file in the Loudoun Papers) : ". . . I immediately set about the Work and has carried it on with great Expedition. The Fort will be extraordinary good, the Indians are highly pleas'd with it as it is much stronger than any they ever saw, the Wall is four foot thick, will be nine Foot high, with Stockade fixed on the Top of the Wall seven feet high, if we meet with no obstructions I shall have it finish'd in twelve or fifteen days. . . . I told them (the Indians) it was expected the Carolina People would Garrison it, but they wou'd not hear of it, they said if the Carolina People built them a Fort they might Garrison it, but should not suffer them to have Possession of the Virginia Fort. . . . Inclos'd Your Hon^r has a List of the Workmen and of what Men Capt Pearis has, some of the best Workmen has two Shillings per Day some others one Shilling & six Pence, thirty four at one Shilling & three Pence. . . . I propose to take a Ride to Keywee which is one hundred and fifty Miles from here. . . . The Carolina People (to aid in building the fort) is not yet arrived, it is my Opinion will not before this Fort is finished. . . ."

When the Cherokee War broke out in 1759, the fort was stoutly besieged by the Indians. Colonel William Byrd of Virginia was dispatched in 1760 with a force to the relief of the garrison but by the end of the year he had got no farther than the Upper Holston, and in disheartenment gave up the attempt. The Indians finally induced the starving party to surrender with a promise of good treatment. The promise was broken and the luckless band of men and women were massacred in characteristic Indian fashion. Some of Daniel Boone's relatives were among the unfortunate party and the account in the Draper collections is a blood-curdling record of the wretched affair. This fort was built by Virginia, because in 1754, and for many years afterward, the southwest boundary of Virginia was still in doubt. All settlements up the Holston and even in Tennessee were regarded as within Virginia territory.

(43) FORT McKENZIE [53]

Fort McKenzie was located on the South Branch of the Potomac. Its exact location has not been ascertained. Captain Robert McKenzie who was stationed here and whose name was given to the fort, commanded the 16th company in the Virginia regiment. Governor Dinwiddie wrote to Captain Robert Stewart, also of the Virginia regiment, December 9, 1757, that he was " glad to hear Cox and Lane got safe in to Captain McKenzie's Fort and their skirmish shows the Necessity of Detachments from all the Forts to be out in Ranging Parties, which at times may probably find some of the enemy in their Lurking Places."

---

[53] Dinwiddie Papers, vol. ii, p. 720; Lewis, p. 211.

(44) McNeil's (or McNeal's) Fort [54]

This defense was situated in eastern present Montgomery County, Virginia, between Fort William and Captain Campbell's Fort, thirteen miles from either. Its garrison was thirty men.

(45) Fort Maddison [55]

Only the fragment of a record of this structure, probably a block-house, has been found, namely, a reference in the Journals of the House of Burgesses to " A Claim of John M'Clanahan, for several Tools which were taken from him for the Use of Fort Maddison, by the Commanding Officer of the said Fort, and never returned to him, appraised to £3.17.6."

(46) Fort Maidstone [56]

Fort Maidstone was a stockade situated along the Potomac River on the bluff on the lower point at the mouth of the Great Cacapon River, in what is now Morgan County, West Virginia. It was forty-five miles from the "'Fort at Parker's" on the South Branch of the Potomac and had at one time a garrison of one hundred and twenty-five men. It is marked on Washington's Map of the Upper Potomac (1756). Governor Dinwiddie instructed Colonel Washington, May 16, 1757, to station Captain Robert Stewart of the Virginia regiment at Fort Maidstone with a garrison of seventy men. This order was carried out, but Washington soon thereafter sent Captain Stewart and his company elsewhere and Governor Dinwiddie later approved this action. Captain Stewart had been at Braddock's defeat, had helped to carry Braddock off the field, and was with the General when he died. Fort Maidstone was considered to be a sufficiently important post to be selected as one of the seven forts to which the

[54] Virginia Magazine of History and Biography, vol. xv, pp. 247-251; Hamilton, vol. ii, pp. 305-307.
[55] Journals, 1761-1765, p. 262.
[56] Sparks, vol. ii, pp. 110, 476; Dinwiddie Papers, vol. ii, pp. 622, 654; Hamilton, vol. i, pp. 280-282, 308, 319-320, 325-328; Lewis, p. 211.

Virginia regiment was distributed at the reorganization of that body in 1757.

(47) FORT AT HUGH MASON'S MILL [57]

The Fort at Hugh Mason's Mill was near Upper Tract, in present Pendleton County, West Virginia.

(48) JOHN MASON'S FORT [58]

John Mason's Fort was situated near present Salem, Roanoke County, Virginia, twenty miles from Voss' Fort, and referred to as " John Mason's on the south side of Roanoke." It had a garrison of thirty men.

(49) MAYO FORT [59]

Mayo Fort was not far from the New River and was the place from which Captain Robert Wade marched with thirty-five men " in order to take a Range to the New River in search of our Enemy Indians."   Hickey's Fort was passed on the way west to the Mayo Fort.

(50) MENDENHALL'S FORT [60]

Three brief references to this place by Washington tell us all that we know of it.   Washington wrote in his memorandum book for April and May, 1756: " This day (May 12) also the King George Militia had orders to march to Mendenhalls Fort to protect the inhabitants under those Mountains."   On May 14 he reported at that fort " Lieut. Thom⁰. with 27 from Orange County."   Again, on May 17 he recorded that " 40 P. M. fm. Caroline " (forty privates from Carolina County) had been substituted for the Orange County contingent there.

---

[57] Virginia Magazine of History and Biography, vol. xv, pp. 247-251.
[58] Ibid., pp. 247-251; Hamilton, vol. i, pp. 306-307.
[59] Summers, pp. 62, 66.
[60] Ford, Writings of Washington, vol. i, pp. 273, 274, 275.

(51) Captain John Miller's Fort [61]

Our records for Captain John Miller's Fort are meagre. The fort stood on Jackson's River between Matthew Harper's Fort and Fort Dinwiddie, about eighteen miles from either. Major Andrew Lewis ordered Captain William Preston, November 23, 1756, to march sixty fresh militia " Draughts " to Miller's Fort and relieve the garrison already there. On August 20, 1757, Daniel Kidd gave a receipt to William Preston for 17s. for seventeen days' work at " Miller's Fort on Jackson's River." The receipt is witnessed by Thomas Lloyd. And on October 5, 1757, John Davies acknowledged the receipt from William Preston of £2 1s. for forty-one days' service as a soldier at Fort Miller. In the same year James Lockhart acknowledged receipt from William Preston of 3s. for three days' labor at Fort Miller. Washington, Colonel Buchanan, and their party visited Miller's Fort in the fall of 1756.

(52) Fort Neally [62]

Fort Neally was a small stockade structure on Opequon River, in what is now Berkeley County, West Virginia. It was attacked and captured at daybreak, September 17, 1756, by a band of Indians who massacred the garrison, and then carried away a number of prisoners from the vicinity. Among these prisoners was Isabella Stockton, a little girl ten years old. Her story, as given by Samuel Kercheval, is as remarkable as it is interesting and romantic. Sometime after her return from captivity she became the wife of Colonel William McCleery, prominent in the early history of Monongalia County. The story of her captivity has been a theme of exciting interest around the firesides of homes in and about Martinsburg for a hundred and fifty years, says Vergil A. Lewis.

---

[61] Virginia Magazine of History and Biography, vol. xv, pp. 247-251; Draper, MSS., Preston Papers, 1QQ137, 6QQ29, 30, 37, 88; Hamilton, vol. i, pp. 305-306.
[62] Lewis, pp. 211-212.

(53) FORT NECESSITY [63]

Fort Necessity, a rude fort, earthen breastworks, hurriedly thrown up, was constructed near the "Crossing of the Youghiogany" by Washington in 1754. The situation of the fort, termed by Washington "a charming field for an encounter," is described in his letter to Governor Dinwiddie from Great Meadows, dated May 27, 1754.[64] Near here Jumonville was killed May 28. The French attacked in force on July 3, 1754, and Washington was obliged to capitulate. The French destroyed the defenses of the place and then returned to their base at Fort Du Quesne.

(54) FORT OHIO [65]

Fort Ohio was a blockhouse situated on the site of the present town of Ridgely, Mineral County, West Virginia. It was built in 1750 as a fortified store-house for the Ohio Company, and stocked with £4000 worth of merchandise purchased in London for the Indian trade on the Ohio. This blockhouse is shown on a sketch map in Winsor's "Narrative and Critical History of America," volume V, page 577, and the "Fort of the Ohio Company" appears on the Fry and Jefferson map of 1751. Governor Dinwiddie wrote Governor Sharpe of Maryland, September 5, 1754, as follows: "I have ordered Colonel Innes to take possession of the Ohio Company's warehouse which will make a very good magazine, and we had better pay rent than begin to build. I have directed a breast work, and the Great Guns to be mounted for Defense; and, if they can build a shed around it, [it] may be proper for the soldiers to lodge in." [66]

(55) PARIS'S FORT [67]

The story of this fort so far we know it is told in one brief reference. Washington records in his memorandum

---

[63] Ford, Writings of Washington, vol. i, pp. 70, 72; see Sparks.
[64] Ford, Writings of Washington, vol. i, pp. 71, 72.
[65] Lewis, p. 212.
[66] Substantially the same account is found in Lewis, p. 212.
[67] Ford, Writings of Washington, vol. i, p. 273.

book, 1756: "May 13th. An express came from Colonel Peyton informing that a Sergeant and 14 men deserted last night from him at Paris's Fort, and desiring Reinforcement. I was obliged to countermand the Orders to the King George Militia and to send them to join him with orders to remain in Ashby's Fort, and they accordingly marched 29 in number under Lieutenant Nugent. The rest were sick & deserted, and this night 4 out of the 29 also marched off."

(56) FORT AT PARKER'S [68]

This defense was situated on the South Branch of the Potomac, ten miles from Fort Ashby on the same stream, and had a garrison of thirty men. A scrap of information in Hamilton's "Letters to Washington" runs, "A Weekly Return of a Company of Rangers Stationed at Parkers Plantation under Command of Capt Cockes 29th Decm^r 1755" shows on that date twenty-seven "totall Effectives."

(57) FORT PATTERSON'S [69]

Fort Patterson's was located on the South Branch of the Potomac. Some mischief was done there in April, 1758, as it was supposed, by two Indians, and Ensign Chew pursued and killed them. Both of the supposed Indians proved to be well-known white men, who had dressed and painted in Indian style, "the more successfully," says Draper, "to plunder and injure their neighbors."

(58) PAUL'S FORT [70]

Paul's Fort was a stockade fort "at the Big spring near to Springfield." The whole Matthews and Maxwell settlement crowded into the fort in 1761, at the time that sixty Shawnese Warriors made an incursion into the settlements on the James River and committed numerous outrages.

---

[68] Ibid., vol. i, p. 372; Hamilton, vol. i, p. 163.
[69] Ford, Writings of Washington, vol. ii, p. 9; Draper, MSS., 1B150; Hamilton, vol. ii, pp. 65, 302, 335.
[70] Withers, p. 68.

(59) FORT PEARSALL [71]

Fort Pearsall (also spelled Pearsal, Pearscall, and Pierce-hall) was a stockade fort built by Job Pearsall on the site of what is now Romney, Hampshire County, West Virginia, at the point where the road from Fort Loudoun west crossed the South Branch. Pearsall was one of the earliest settlers on the South Ranch. " Pearsall's " is shown on Washington's map of Operations in Virginia, 1756. In the year 1754, Fort Pearsall was the chief base of supplies in Virginia on the south side of the Upper Potomac, says Lewis. In December of that year, Governor Dinwiddie ordered " all the garrisons of the Branch to evacuate their forts, and repair to Pearsall's," but this order was almost immediately countermanded. Captain Thomas Cocks' Journal in 1755 says that he marched from Winchester, September 8, reached " Piercehalls on South Branch " on the 11th, " lay there " the 12th, and " march'd to Hedges Patterson Creek " on the 13th, which gives one a general idea of the location with references to other places. Fort Pearsall was considered an important place, and when the Virginia regiment was reduced in size in 1757, Governor Dinwiddie instructed Colonel Washington, May 16, 1757, to station a garrison of forty-five men under Captain Robert McKenzie, at the fort. A month later, Lieutenant James Livingston wrote to Washington that he was endeavoring to halt friendly Indians at that place.

(60) FORT PETERSON [72]

Fort Peterson was a small stockade fort situated on the South Branch of the Potomac, two miles above the mouth of the North Branch in what is now Grant County, West Virginia. In 1756, the year in which provision was made for its erection, the northern boundary line of Augusta County passed through the mouth of the North Fork of the

[71] Hamilton, vol. i, p. 267; vol. ii, pp. 72, 96, 321; vol. iii, p. 89; Lewis, pp. 212-213; Ford, Writings of Washington, vol. i, pp. 274, 275; vol. ii, pp. 40, 41, 42; Journals, 1761-1765, p. 114.
[72] J. A. Waddell, Annals of Augusta County, p. 90; Virginia Magazine of History and Biography, vol. xv, pp. 247-251.

South Branch, and all the valley of that river above that point lay in Augusta County. July 27, 1756, in compliance with an order of Governor Dinwiddie, a council of war was held at Augusta Court House,—now Staunton,—and it was unanimously resolved to erect a fort "at Peterson's on the South Branch of Potomack nigh Mill Creek," two miles from the northern county line.

(61) FORT PLEASANT [73]

Fort Pleasant was a strong defense, having cabins, palisades, and blockhouses. It was situated on the "Indian Old Fields" about a mile and a half above the "Trough" on the South Branch of the Potomac, in present Hardy County, West Virginia, twenty miles from Fort Defiance on the same stream. It was erected by Captain Thomas Waggoner under orders from Colonel Washington in 1756. It had a garrison of sixty men. In its earlier years, it was frequently called, from its builder, Fort Van Meter, and later, after the founding of Moorefield, was often referred to as the "Town Fort" because of its proximity to it. "Fort Pleasant" is shown on Washington's map of "Operations in Virginia," 1756. Samuel Kercheval, the historian, visited the site in 1830 when "one of the block-houses, with port-holes was still standing, and the logs particularly sound." Around it was long a scene of barbarous warfare. Within a mile and a half, and in sight of its walls was fought, in 1756, the "Battle of the Trough," one of the bloodiest contests ever waged between the white and red men in the valley of the South Branch. The garrison from Fort Pleasant was largely slaughtered. The best account of this action is that written by Felix Renick and published in the "American Pioneer," Cincinnati, 1843. Another good account is that written by Dr. Charles Turley and printed in Kercheval's "History of the Valley," (1833), pages 98 and 100. An account of another bloody tragedy not far from Fort Pleas-

[73] Ford, Writings of Washington, vol. i, p. 372; Kercheval (1st ed.), pp. 96, 98, 99, 100, 101, 109, 122, 123; Washington's Journal of 1784, ed. by Hulbert, pp. 78, 79; Felix Renick, article in the American Pioneer, 1843, vol. ii, pp. 38, 39, 40; Lewis, pp. 213-214.

ant is that of James S. Miles also given by Kercheval, page 101. Many other stirring scenes were enacted in this vicinity. George Washington was on the " Indian Old Fields " in 1747-1748, when surveying land for Lord Fairfax, and again visited the spot September 29, 1784, when Fort Pleasant appears to have been still standing.

(62) POWELL'S FORT [74]

Powell's Fort was a small fort about fifteen miles from Painter's fortified house in the neighborhood of Mill Creek, about nine miles south of what is now Woodstock, Virginia. Keller's Fort was near enough to send to it for aid.

(63) FORT RIDDLE [75]

Fort Riddle was a small stockade fort on Lost River, in Hardy County, West Virginia. Near it, in the spring of 1756, a fierce and bloody battle was fought at the head of Capon River between a body of fifty Indians commanded by a French captain, and a company of twenty Virginia frontiersmen under Captain Jeremiah Smith. The Indians were defeated, Captain Smith killing the French officer with his own hands. He had in his possession a commission and instructions directng him to attack Fort Frederick in Maryland. A man named Chesmer was later killed by Indians at this fort.

(64) FORT ROBINSON [76]

Fort Robinson was situated on the northern bank of Holston River and nearly opposite the upper end of the Long Island. It was built by Colonel Adam Stephen, 1760.

(65) FORT SELLERS [77]

Fort Sellers was a small stockade on the east side of Patterson's Creek and about four miles from the Potomac, in

[74] De Haas, p. 205; Kercheval (ed. of 1833), p. 135.

[75] Ibid., pp. 93, 115; De Haas, p. 204; Lewis, p. 214.

[76] Draper, MSS., 2B108.

[77] Sparks, vol. ii, pp. 110, 125, 145; Washington's Journal, 1747-1748, ed. by Toner, p. 42, 1754, p. 69; Lewis, pp. 214-215.

Mineral County, West Virginia, where Washington surveyed lands for Elias Sellers, April 1, 1748. Later, Washington built this fort and referring to it in his letter to Governor Dinwiddie, April 22, 1756, said, " A small fort which we have at the mouth of Patterson's Creek, containing an officer and thirty men guarding stores, was attacked suddenly by French and Indians; they were warmly received, upon which they retired." It is shown on Washington's map of " Operations in Virginia," 1756.

(66) Fort Seybert [78]

Fort Seybert [79] was a strong fort, having cabins, palisades, and blockhouses. It stood on the South Fork of the South Branch of the Potomac, twelve miles northeast of the present Franklin, in Pendleton County, West Virginia. " It was besieged by Indians April 28, 1758, the attack continuing for three days. Thirty persons were in the fort; after two Indians had been killed, the garrison surrendered with the promise that the lives of all should be spared. The promise was broken. The savages rushed in, bound ten, and then twenty of the captives were seated in a row on a log, with an Indian standing behind each, who at a given signal sunk his tomahawk into the head of his victim; an additional blow or two dispatched them. The others were carried into captivity. Among them was James Dyer, then fourteen years of age. Two years later he escaped from his captors when in the Scioto Valley and returned home. A son of his, Colonel Zebulon Dyer, was long Clerk of the Court of Pendleton County, West Virginia. The Indians burned the fort, but it was rebuilt by order of the Virginia Assembly. The attack was made on this fort the day after the massacre at Fort Upper Tract, Pendleton County."

(67) Fort Shepherd [80]

Fort Shepherd was on the south bank of the Potomac

---

[78] Kercheval, James Dyer's account, pp. 120, 121; Hening, vol. vii, p. 180; Howe, p. 428; DeHaas, p. 208 (see DeHaas for an illustration of this fort); Withers, pp. 65-67; Peyton, pp. 116-117.
[79] Called by Withers, " Fort Sivert," p. 65ff.
[80] Mrs. Danske Dandridge, Historic Shepherdstown, p. 28.

River, near Old Pack Horse Ford, where Shepherdstown, Jefferson County, West Virginia, now stands. It was a stone house, stockaded, on the site of the present Shepherd College State Normal.

(68) STEPHEN'S FORT [81]

Stephen's Fort stood on Cedar Creek, ten or fifteen miles from Major Robert White's Fort near the Capon River in the North Mountain neighborhood. On this spot Zane's iron works were afterwards set up. It was the refuge of the Fawcett and other families near it after the massacre in June, 1764, of the people near White's Fort.

(69) CAPTAIN TERRY'S FORT [82]

This defense was situated on " Black water," twenty-six miles from Captain Galloway's Fort on Smith's River, and an equal distance from Captain Hog's Fort on the Roanoke, and had allotted to it a garrison of twenty men. Under the name of Blackwater Fort, probably the same place, the minutes of the House of Burgesses mention " A Petition of Joseph Rentfro, praying to be allowed for a Horse impressed by Capt. John Blagg to carry an Express from Blackwater Fort to Fredericksburg, for his Majesty's, which was never returned to him, and for which he hath not received any Satisfaction, was presented to the House and read."

(70) FORT TRIAL [83]

Fort Trial was on Smith's River and was the " most southerly of the forts."

(71) FORT AT TROUT ROCK [84]

The Fort at Trout Rock was four miles south of present

[81] Kercheval, ed. of 1833, p. 133.

[82] Ford, Writings of Washington, vol. i, p. 372; Journals, 1761-1765, p. 261.

[83] Virginia Magazine of History and Biography, vol. xv, pp. 248-249.

[84] Ibid., Ford, Writings of Washington, vol. i, pp. 371-373.

Franklin, West Virginia, and the name is still preserved. Its garrison was fixed at from fifty to seventy-five men. Washington, in his Plan of Forts, drawn up in the fall of 1756, locates it on the South Branch, but lists it at that time as " not built."

(72) UNKNOWN FORT [85]

Samuel Kercheval, in his History of the Valley, mentions a fort on the South Branch of the Potomac, seven miles above Romney and another fort as standing eight miles above the same town. He gives a name to neither; they were probably one and the same. Two Indian boys appeared before the fort some time in 1757, or therebouts, whereupon a party from the fort started out to capture them. An Indian warrior made his appearance also and was shot down by Shadrack Wright. An ambuscade had been prepared by the Indians with the result that a few of those who had gone forth from the garrison were killed.

(73) FORT UPPER TRACT [86]

Fort Upper Tract, a stockade, was erected in 1756 under the direction of Colonel Washington. It stood a short distance west of the South Branch of the Potomac at what is now known as " Upper Tract," Pendleton County, West Virginia. Colonel Washington writing Governor Dinwiddie on January 14, 1756, concerning the building of forts in the valley of the South Branch, says: " I have now ordered Captain Waggoner with sixty men to build and garrison two others (forts) at places I have pointed out high up the South Branch." Writing the governor further on the same subject, under date of August 14, ensuing, he said: " We

---

[85] Kercheval (ed. of 1833), p. 102; Lewis, p. 217.
[86] Virginia Gazette, May 5, 1756; Ford, Writings of Washington, vol. i, p. 325; vol. ii, pp. 125, 179; W. A. Crozier, Virginia Colonial Militia, p. 18; Preston's " Manuscript Register " of persons killed, wounded and captured by Indians between 1754 and 1758, found in the Draper, MSS.; " Notes of Lyman C. Draper," printed on p. 87 of Thwaites' Edition of Withers' Chronicles of Border Warfare; Dinwiddie Papers, vol. ii, p. 316; Lewis, pp. 215-216.

have built some forts and altered others as far south on the Potomac waters as any settlers have been molested; and there only remains one body of inhabitants, at a place called Upper Tract, who need a guard. Thither I have ordered a party," —that is, a small garrison. The officer placed in command was Captain James Dunlap, of Augusta County, who in 1756, had commanded a company in the Big Sandy Expedition. All went well here until April 27, 1758, when it was attacked by French and Indians, who captured and burned the fort, and Captain Dunlap and twenty-two others were killed. The next day, the same party laid siege to Fort Seybert and massacred the inmates there, as related in connection with that fort. Washington, at the time, placed the loss at " about sixty persons killed and missing " at the two forts. This defense was the same as Fort Upper Settlement, mentioned in Ford's Writings of Washington.[87]

(74) VOSS' FORT [88]

Voss' Fort stood on the headwaters of the Roanoke River, in old Augusta County, about ten miles west of present Christiansburg, Virginia. Washington says it was " 60 miles from Luney's Ferry on the James River." The name is spelled variously Vaulx, Vause, Vauss, Vaux, and Vauces. This defense was strongly built and guarded an important pass. It was the nearest place of refuge for settlers on the New River. Andrew Lewis (?) wrote to Governor Dinwiddie (?) that on the 26th of June, 1756, a large body of Indians took the fort, burned it, and killed the inmates, twenty-four hours before aid was at hand. Andrew Lewis wrote further to Governor Dinwiddie in June, 1756:

Captain Ephraim Vause has been a very great Sufferer by the late unhappy affair, his Wife & two Daughters two Servants & one

---

[87] Vol. i, p. 372.
[88] Ford, Writings of Washington, vol. i, pp. 356, 442; Sparks, vol. ii, p. 190; Virginia Magazine of History and Biography, vol. xv, pp. 247-251; Summers, pp. 57, 58, 62; Johnston, p. 32; Journals, 1756-1758, pp. 439, 454, 458, 501, 502, 505; 1758-1761, pp. 221, 229; Draper, MSS., Preston Papers, 1QQ131-135, 8ZZ49; Hamilton, vol. i, pp. 306-307, 347; vol. ii, pp. 15, 48, 53, 57, 72, 96.

Negro all either killed or taken Prisoners, his Fort (Raised at his own Expense) and Barn with the other Buildings on his Planta- tion Burned to Ashes and above eighty heads of Cattle & Horses killed and Carried away. . . .

Lewis strongly advised that Voss' Fort be rebuilt. This was done, Captain Peter Hog having charge of the work. The plans called for a fort one hundred feet square in the clear, with stockades at least ten feet high. It was to be garrisoned by seventy men. Dinwiddie thought that even three forts would not be too many for such an important section of the frontier. Hale gives a brief account of Mrs. Ingles' presentiment that the fort would be attacked, of her husband's removal of her to " another Fort . . . down be- low the Blue Ridge, and not far from the ' Peaks of Otter,' " and of the early destruction of the fort.

(75) FORT WARDEN [89]

Fort Warden (sometimes spelled Wardon) was a small stockade fort that stood not far from the present town of Wardensville, Hardy County, West Virginia. Near this place on November 11, 1749, Washington surveyed for Wil- liam Warden, the builder of the fort, " a certain tract of waste and ungranted land." And at this place, in 1758, William Warden and a Mr. Taff were killed by Indians who burned the fort.

(76) FORT WASHINGTON [90]

We know little of Fort Washington except that David Robinson wrote " from the Fort on Catawba " to William Preston, September 14, 1755 : " Mr. Stringham has returned from Fort Washington once more, and now assumes to him- self the title of Captain, however we have metamorphosed him into a common soldier, until you return."

---

[89] Washington's Journal, 1747-1748, ed. by Toner, p. 87; Ker- cheval, p. 115; DeHaas, p. 204; Lewis, p. 216.
[90] Journals, 1756-1758, p. 504; Draper, MSS., Preston Papers, 1QQ88.

(77) WHITE'S FORT [91]

White's Fort was a small fort, or palisaded house, built by Major Robert White, and stood near the Capon River. It was an asylum in times of danger for people of the North Mountain neighborhood. Near here Owen Thomas, who was riding about the vicinity to warn the settlers of an Indian attack, was shot and scalped in July, 1763. Near here also in June of the following year twenty-two or twenty-three persons belonging to the Jones and Clouser families were killed, wounded, or taken prisoners. The escape of Mrs. Thomas, widow of Owen Thomas, is both interesting and remarkable. It is related by Kercheval in his History of the Valley.

(78) FORT WILLIAM [92]

Fort William stood on the Catawba Branch of the James River, thirty-six miles from Captain Hog's Fort on the Roanoke River and in present Botetourt County, Virginia. Washington allotted to it a garrison of seventy-five men. As we know, Washington made an inspection of the Virginia Frontier forts in the fall of 1756. Writing from Halifax to Governor Dinwiddie, October 10, 1756, Washington informed him that Captain Preston had conducted him to Colonel Buchanan's house at Luney's Ferry and that Colonel Buchanan told him with very grave concern, " that it was not in his power to raise men; for that, three days before, some of the militia in a fort (Fort William) about fifteen miles above his house, at the head of Catawba Creek, commanded by one Colonel Nash, were attacked by the Indians, which occasioned all that settlement to break up totally, even as far as the ferry at Luney's (on James River); that he had ordered three companies to repair thither, and march against the enemy, and not one man came, except a captain, lieutenant, and seven or eight men from Bedford." Fort William stood guard over an important point. Andrew Lewis

---

[91] Kercheval (ed. of 1833), pp. 130-133.
[92] Sparks, vol. ii, pp. 190-191; Draper, MSS., Preston Papers, 1QQ131-133; 1QQ88, 146.

wrote to Governor Dinwiddie (?) in June, 1756, that he had "Ordered Capt. Christian with a Company to take Possession of Fort William, which was built by Captain Preston in a very convenient Pass. . . ." From "Fort on Catawba" (Fort William) David Robinson wrote William Preston (?) on October 14, 1755, describing conditions on the frontier. The Preston Papers also contain a statement of an account against "The Country" for provisions delivered at Fort William in Augusta County, Virginia. The account is filed by William Ralston.

(79) FORT WILLIAMS [93]

Fort Williams was a stockade fort situated on the South Branch of the Potomac two miles below Hanging Rock, Hampshire County, West Virginia. In July, 1764, a party of Delaware Indians having made an entry into settlements about Cedar Creek returned with a number of prisoners to the South Branch and encamped close to Hanging Rock. A party of men on their way back to Fort Williams discharged their rifles. This action frightened the Indians and they hastened across the river, carrying their prisoners with them as best they could. Mrs. Owen Thomas, one of the victims, was carried down stream by the current, and having lodged against a rock she climbed on top of it and remained in that situation all night. The following morning she escaped to the shore, made her way to Fort Williams, and from there taken to her home, only to find it had been burned, and to learn that her neighbors and several of her children had fallen victims of the Indians.

(80) FORT WILSON [94]

Fort Wilson was a small defense built on the Bull Pasture River, a gathering place in times of alarm for the people who lived in the vicinity. Major Andrew Lewis ordered

---

[93] The account by Major John White is given in Kercheval (ed. of 1833), pp. 130-131; Lewis, pp. 216-217.

[94] Draper, MSS., Preston Papers, 1QQ137.

Preston, November 23, 1756, to leave " a sergt. and twelve men at Wilson's Fort in the Bull Pasture."

(81) FORT YOUNG [95]

According to Withers, Fort Young was located on Jackson River. This historian speaks of the " weakness of this fort." Our information about Fort Young is meager although the Preston Papers contain a few references to it. Lewis wrote to Preston on October 28, 1757, that he would shortly arrive at Fort Young. From Preston's reply to him the next day it is inferred that Lewis had to pass Captain Dunlap's Fort on his way to Fort Young. The Journals of the House of Burgesses mention " A Petition of Arthur Campbell, setting forth that on the 14th of September, 1758, he joined a Company of Rangers, under the command of Capt. John Dickenson, stationed at Fort Young in Augusta County."

---

[95] Ibid., 1QQ162-163; Journals, 1761-1765, pp. 254, 324.

APPENDIX II

No. 1

REPORT FROM GOVERNOR DINWIDDIE ON THE PRESENT STATE OF VIRGINIA

Transmitted the Lords Commissioners for Trade and Plantations, January, 1755.

The Boundaries of the Dom'n of Virg'a, as they were first established by the Charter of King James the 1st, Anno. 1606, were from Cape Comfort, now called Cape Henry, 200 Miles North along the Sea Coast, and the same Distance South from the same Cape, and West to the So. Sea, together with all Islands in both Seas, lying within 100 Miles of the Main Land; in w'ch Tract is comprehended (a) great Part of y't w'ch is now called No. Carolina, all the Province of M'yl'd, and part of Pennsylvania. But the Boundaries of Virg'a, as it is now circumscribed, are to the East and So. East, the main Atlantick Ocean, on the South, a due West line from the Mouth of Curratuck Inlet, w'ch lies in the Lat. of 36 D., and 30M, divides Virg'a from No. Car., and on the No., a Line from the Sea, thro' y't Isthmus called the E. Shore to the Bay of Chesapeake opposite to y't Point of Potowmack River called Watkins's Point, which lies in Lat. 38; and thence, the s'd River Potowmack divides this Colony from Maryl'd unto the true Meridian of the first Fountain of Potowmack, w'ch is the utmost Boundary of M'yl'd Westward. And then Virg'a resumes its ancient Breadth, and has not other Limits to the West y'n w't its first Royal Charter assigned it, and y't is to the So. Sea, including the Isl'd of California, but, according to its Breadth from the West Line, w'ch divides it from No. Car. on the So., to the first Fount'n of Potowmack on the No., it will extend on the Western side of M'yl'd as far as the Latitude of 40 No. and So., northerly on the Back of Pennsylvania. The Situat'n is under the same Paralel with some of the finest Countrys in the World, and undoubtedly to Co'try is capable of the same Product's as the Fertility of the Soil is equal to any of them since, with Little Labour, every Thing is propagated w'ch the Planter has attempted. The Air is temperate; the extreme Heat in Sumer, or Cold in Winter, is but of short D'ration, as they are frequently relieved with intervening cold, and warm Breezes. The Western Boundary as yet is not well known, nor can it be expected to be fully known for some Ages. The British Subjects have for some years settled within a few Miles of the River Ohio, on the other side of the Allagany Mount's, w'ch settlem't was approved of by the Ind's, and a Grant of the Land was made to H. M'y, the K. of G. B., by the Six Nat's at the Treaty of Lancaster. These settlem'ts I was willing to fix as our pres't Boundary to the Westw'd, as it is part of the Lands belonging to the five Nat's, w'ch, by the Treaty of Utritch, is expressly allowed to be under the Dom'n of the Crown of G. B., and as further, the Lake Champlain, formerly called Lake Iroq(u)ois, and the Co'try So'w'd of it, as also the Lakes Ontario and Erie have, by all ancient authors, both Fr. and English, been

149

allowed to belong to the five Nat's of Ind's, and in Course, by the above Treaty, to be under the Protec'n of the B. Crown. Notwithstand'g the above Treaty, the Fr. have, subsequent thereto, built several Forts on the Lands belong'g to the Five Nat's, and a remarkable strong one at Crown Point to the So'w'd of Lake Champlain. The Treaty of Aix la Chapelle, confirm'g the Treaty of Utritch, has no weight with the Fr., but it appears y't the Conquest of ye whole Cont't seems to be the object of their Attent'n. The Fr., since the above Treaties, have erected many Fortresses on the Lands belong'g to the Five Nat's, who are actually under the Protect'n of G. B., and contrary to Law and Justice, erect these Forts as the Marks of Possess'n, and they have been constantly increasing their Forces by importing Numbers of People from France in a Private Manner, not to be notic'd, or observed by the Powers of Europe. They have, for the last seven years, robb'd our Subjects, trading with the Ind's in our back Co'try, and sent their Persons Prisoners to Quebeck, all w'ch is a most notorious Infract'n of the above Treaties. Not satisfied with these clandestine and Private Robberies, they have now taken off the Mask, and y's last Sumer declared, in this part of the World, y'r Intent's. I was ordered by H. M'y to build some Forts on His Lands on the River Ohio. In Obedience therto, I ordered out some Soldiers and Tradesmen to begin a Fort on the Forks of Monongahela, till I was qualified by our Assembly to send stronger Forces to y't Fort, and to build some others. The Fr., with an armed Force from Canada, came down the River Ohio, surpriz'd our People, took Possess'n of His M'y's Forts, and robbed and plundered all our poor settlers y't were hear to y't River, some of whom had lived peacibly there upwards of 10 Years. I raised w't Men the small Pittance our Assembly granted in Feb'y last, enabled me to do, who, with an Independ't Co'y H. M'y was pleased to order from So. Car., on their march to the Ohio, were attacked by the Fr. and Ind's, with a much superior Force, many of our Men were killed and the rest obliged to such a Capitulat'n as their inferiority of numbers and the situat'n of their Affairs compelled them to comply with. These Transact's in the Time of tranquil Peace between the Two Crowns, I conceive is with't Preced't, and I am convinc'd there is no conduct'g an Expedition with't Aid from Home, and an Act of the B. Parliam't to oblige the Colonies to raise Money for their own Protec'n. But to ret'n to the present State of Virg'a. The establish'd Constitut'n of the Gov't of Virg'a is as follows: A chief Gov'r, appointed by His M'y who always resides in G. B.; A L't Gov'r, appointed also by H. M'y, who presides over the Affairs of Gov't; A Council, consist'g of 12 Gent'n, appointed by Mandamus from H. M'y. The Dom'n has now 50 Counties, who elect two Members for each co'ty; one for the College of W. and M'y, one for the City of W'msb'g, one for Jas. Town, and one for the Borough of Norfolk, in all 104 Memb'rs, who are called at Meet'g, the Ho. of Burgesses. The Lieut. Gov'r, Council, and Ho. of Burgesses, are the Gen'l Assembly of this Colony, and are impowered to enact Acts for the good Gov't of the Co'try. These Acts are duly transmitted to G. B., soon after each Session, for His M'y's Assent and Approbation; w'n they receive H. M'y's Sanc't they become Laws. The administrat'n of Justice. First, There are in each Co'ty, Courts held monthly by Persons commissioned by the Gov'r, who have not only the Power of Justices of the Peace, but have Cognizance of all Suits, of w't value so ever, arising within their respective Jurisdict's, both at Comon Law and in Chancery, except only such criminal Offences as are punishable with the Loss of Life or Member.   And for the City of W'msburg, there is a Court of Hustings held Monthly, before the Mayor, Recorder and Aldermen, for all Suits at comon Law aris'g within the Town, hav'g equal Jurisdiction in all Suits at Comon Law with the County Courts.   There is the like Court in the Bor'o of Norfolk; these are the inferior Courts in this Gov't, and from their Judgem't, an Appeal lies to the Gen'l Court. The Appellant giving Security to prosecute the same with effect. The Gen'l Court consists of the Gov'r and Members of the Council, any five whereof make a Quorum; this Court is held in Apr. and Oct'r, and has Jurisdict'n of all Causes, real, Personal and mixt, at comon Law, bro't hither, originally exceeding the Value of £10 Sterling, or by Appeal or Supersedeas (w'ch is in the Nature of a Writ of Error) from the Inferior Courts, all Criminal Offences are here tryable, and it is also a Court of Chancery for matters of great Value.   But, by a late Act of Assembly, no Appeal or Supersedeas lies from the Judgem't or Decree of any inferior Court, unless the Debt or Damage, or Thing in dem'd (exclusive of the Costs) exceeds the Value of 5£; Except'g only where the Title or Bounds of Lands are in Question, and from the Gen'l Court an Appeal lies to the King and Council in any Causes of 300£ St'g and upwards; Secondly, There are two Courts of oyer and terminer held Yearly, the one the second Friday in June, the other the second Tuesday in Dec'r, wherein all Criminals y't happen to be committed after the respective Gen'l Courts, are tried.   The Judges here, are only such as are Members of the Council, and sit by the Governor's Commiss'n, pursuant to H. M'y's Instruct's in y't behalf; Thirdly, For the punishm't of Slaves committ'g Cappital Crimes, a Com'o. of Oyer and Terminer is issued by the Gov'r, directed to the Justices of the Peace in the Co'y where the offence is comitted, to try the Offenders, on Proof of the Fact by Witnesses, with't any Jury, and on Convict'n, the Commiss'rs award Execution, and set a Value on the Slave, w'ch Valuat'n is afterwards p'd the Owner by the Gen'l Assembly as an Encourage-ment to the People to discover the Villain(ie)s of their Slaves; Fourthly, For Breaches of the Acts of Trade, and for determin'g Controversies concern'g Mariners' Wages, and all Maratime Affairs, there is a Court of Ad'lty, held before a Judge Constituted by Comiss'n under the Seal of the High Court of Ad(mira)lty of G't B'n.   And to this Court belongs an Advocate, Register, and a Mar-shall, appointed by the Gov'r, who is also by Com'o. Vice Admiral of all the Sea Coasts, Rivers and Creeks within this Gov't.   This Court is not held at any certain Time, but is called and held, as Business or Occasion may require, and from this Court an Appeal lies to the King in Council.   The Gov'r sh'd have a Com'o for trying Pyrates; none such to be found here, tho' I am informed my Predecessor had such a Comiss'n.   There is a Court of Comis-sary of the Bishop of London, w'ch only relates to the Punishm't of the Imoralities of the Clergy, and proceeds by Monition, Sus-pension, or Deprivation, as the Nature of the Offence deserves, and from thence there lies an Appeal to the Delegates appointed by His M'y's Comiss'n in England.   Having treated of the Courts of Jus-tice of this Gov't, it may not be improper to mention here how His M'y's Mercy is dispensed to Offenders who are proper Objects thereof; and herein, such is the grace and Favo. of the Crown, y't the Gov'r is invested with a Power to pardon all Crimes and Offences, Treason and willful Murder only excepted, and in these he has a Power of reprieving, untill, on a fair Represent'n of the Circumstances of the Fact, the King is pleased to signify His Com'ds for pardoning or executing the Sentence.

The Gov'r has also a Power to remit all Fines and Forfeitures occurring to the Crown, under the Value of 10£ St'g, and if above, he may suspend the levying such Fines and Forfeitures untill H(is) M'y's Pleasure is known, but this Indulgence does not reach to the Inhabitants of the No'ern Neck, the Fines, &c., being granted to L'd Fairfax, the Proprietor thereof. Thus much for the Civil Constitut'n of this Dom'n, so far as relates to the making and Execut'g the Laws and the Administrat'n of Justice. For matters of State, there is a Council appointed by the King, to be assisting to the Gov'r in all Things relating to the King's Service, such as the disposing of his Lands, the managing his Revenue, the appoint'g of Justices of the Peace, Sheriff, and Coroners, and other Officers of Trust, who receive their Commiss's from the Gov'r.

(They are also) for the better ordering the Tributary Ind's, and mak'g War or Peace with foreign Ind's and Nat's, and various other Matters w'ch Concern the Publick Peace of the Gov't, and w'ch do not fall under the Direct'n of positive Laws.

The trade of this Colony is principally conducted in Ships from G. B. I suppose not less y'n 120 Sail are here annually, with the Produce of y's Dom'n. The Trade exclusive of the above, consists of about sixty Sail, Ships, Scows, Brigantines, Schooners and Sloops, w'ch are navigated by 500 Sailors, besides the small Shallops, w'ch are constantly employ'd in transport'g the Comodities from our River, and in loading the Ships bound for G. B. The Trade in general has greatly increas'd for the last 10 Years and (is) chiefly supported, as to the Shipping, with Cordage, Sail Cloth, &c., from Home. The People in y's Dom'n are supplied from G. B. with all sorts of Woolen Manufactories such as B'd Cloth, Kersey, Duffills, Cottons, Crepes, Ruggs, Blankets, Norwich and other Stuffs, Hatts, Stocks, Shoes, and all sorts of Linens, British, Irish and Gurnsey, all sorts of Household Furniture, and wear'g apparel, with Calicoes, Persians and other East India Goods; Sail Duck, Cordage, with all manner of Iron Ware, as Locks, Hinges, Nails, Carpenter's, Joiner's and Smith's Tools, Axes, Hoes, Anchors, Fire-Arms. With Wines, Spices, Fruits, Loaf-Sugar, and Strong Beer, and other Family Necessaries amo't'g to, by Comput'n 300,000(£) St'g. The Trade from y's (Colony) is chiefly to G. B. and the B. Colonies; some Times, Staves, Wheat, and Indian Corn to Lisbon and the Islands of Maderia. From Lisbon, the Remittances are made to G. B. From Maderia, they have Wine for their Goods. The Produce of this Co'try, and its amo. may be computed, as follows:

50,000 Hhds. of Tob'o [1] @ 4£ per Hhd. N't,......£200,000
10,000 bbls. Pitch and Tar @ 8s.,...............   4,000

---

[1] The export of Tobacco for the period 1750-1756 were: 1750, 48,567; 1751, 46,703; 1752, 48,380; 1753, 59,847; 1754, 50,803; 1755, 47,687; 1756, 28,452 hogsheads.

4,000	Tons Pig Iron @ £5.....................	20,000
	Deer Skins and Furs....................	20,000
40,000	Bush's Wheat @ 2s. 6d..................	5,000
250,000	do. Indian Corn @ 12d................	12,500
10,000	lbs. Bees-Wax @ 12d..................	500
30,000	lbs. Beef and Pork @ 40s..............	60,000
	Pipe Head'g, bl. Staves with Shingles.....	10,000
	Snake Root, Jenzang,[2] &c...............	2,000

$$£334,000$$

This Colony has no Trade with any foreign Plant's except to some of the Dutch Islands of St. Eustatia, and Curracoa; from thence, they some Times smuggle in some Fr. Sugars and Rum. To prevent this, the Collectors and Nav'l Officers are directed to be very careful in inspect'g their Clearances, and search'g their Vessels, but the Co'try is so Extensive, with many Creeks and Bays, y't they run their Goods before they come to Enter at the Custom Ho., but I cannot learn y't much collusive Trade is carried on from this Com'n. There are large quantities of Iron Oar in many Places, and some Furnaces[3] for manufacturing it, fit to send to G. B.; some Appearances of Copper,[4] but for want of proper Persons acquainted with Minerals, the People don't prosecute their Searches with Spirit. There are also Tin, Lead, and Antimony in several Places near the Great Mount's, and, I doubt not, other rich Minerals; but (for) the want of Persons of Knowledge, and (of) Monied Men, these Discoveries must be Dormant for some Time.

The Number of Inhabitants, from the most exact Acc'ts I can have, of White and Black, are 230,000, and the(y) Annually increase in Numbers. There are 50 Counties, each has a Co'ty Lt., Colo., Lieut .Colo. and Major, and according to the largeness of the Co'ty, their Militia is divided into Compa's, each Company hav'g a Capt., Lieut. and Ensign, and our Militia may now amo. to 27,000 Men from 21 to 60 Years of Age. In order to bring the Militia into good Discipline, and a proper Use of their Arms, I divided this Dom'n into four Districts, and appointed experienc'd

---

[2] Ginseng.

[3] There were in operation in Virginia, in September, 1732, four furnaces for the manufacture of iron, viz; one at Fredericksville, twenty-five miles south of Fredericksburg, of which Colonel Chiswell was manager; the works of Ex-Governor Spotswood, at Germanna, in Orange county, twenty miles southwest of Fredericksburg; English works on the north side of the Rappahannock river, in King George county, and the Accokeek furnace, in which Lawrence Washington was interested, in Stafford county. The three first were visited by Colonel William Byrd, at the period stated, and he gives interesting particulars regarding the manufactures, value, etc., of iron. It commanded in England £3 per ton, of which the expense for freights and other charges was 30s., leaving a net yield of £4 10s. Westover MSS. (ed. of 1866), "Progress to the Mines," vol. ii, p. 50ff.

[4] Colonel Byrd also mentions, in 1733, mines of Copper, Lead and Silver, on the south side of James river. One of the first was operated by Drury Stith (ibid., "Journey to Land of Eden," p. 3 ff.).

Persons to be Adjutants, to teach the officers, and y'n the private Men their Exercises, w'ch I hope, will in Time bring the Militia into good Order and Discipline; for our whole Dependence (under God) must be on them, for we have no Forts in y's Dom'n. There was one erected at the mouth of Jas. River, but as it was built on a Sandy Foundat'n, the Sea and Weather destroy'd it, (so) y't the Guns lie dismounted, and (are) of no Use. There are two small Batteries on York River, (which) are only of Service to protect the Merch't Ships in y't River, and (are) of no Defence ag'st an Enemy y't have Force sufficient to attack them by Land, or a Ship Force to run up the River, may demolish them both. And I wish the Colony was in good Circumstances to build Forts of some better Materials than Wood; but the small Funds w'ch the Assembly here is able to raise, are not equal to so considerable an Undertaking; and in War, with't some of H. M'y's Ships of War, y's Domin'n w'd be subject to the insults of small Privateers. This is highly worthy of (the most) serious considerat'n. (Of the) Indians: The tributary Ind's, subject to the Rules of this Gov't, are much reduced and very inconsiderable; there are at pres't only the Pamunkey [5] and Nottaways, their Numbers together, are not above 60 fight'g Men, they are seated among the Inhabit'ts and live in Peace and Amity with them. The other Nat's of Ind's y't are near us, and profess Fr'dship and League with the English, are the Six Nat's to the No'wards, the Catawbas, Cherokees, Chickasaws, and Creeks to the So'w'd. The different Nat's on the River Ohio, the Picts, Twightwees, and Shawnesse to the Westw'd, if they be not seduced by the Fr., who are between Us and them. This Colony has always been happy, and in firm Peace with the Ind's till lately, the Fr. have, by Threats and fair Promises, seduced some of the Ind's from the B. Interest, and with great injustice invaded H. M'y's Lands, plundered and Robbed many of his Subjects, and carried many of them to Quebec. The Fr. do not make regular Settlements, but build Fortresses as marks of Possession, with't Justice or any Shadow of Right to the Lands where they build their Forts, and make incursions among our frontier Settlem'ts (who lie scattered for the Benefit of the best Lands) and rob them of their Cattle, Corn, &c., and often murder

---

[5] A treaty appears to have been made with the Pamunkey and Chickahominy Indians some little time prior to 1753, as by an Enactment provided in the Randolph and in the Bland MSS. Laws, and incorporated by Hening, as of such date, "the commissioners of York are required that such persons as are seated upon the land of Pamunkey or Chickahominy Indians, be removed, according to a late act of Assembly made to that purpose" (Hening, vol. i, p. 380). A small settlement of the descendants of the Pamunkey Indians, combining with the original blood that of the white and negro races, still exists on the Pamunkey river, in King William county, with ancient immunity from taxation. Their interests are represented by trustees appointed by the State Assembly, who are also the arbitrators of all disputes arising among them, which their chosen chief, or local magistrate, may be unable to adjudicate. They have the benefit of Christian ministration, and a school is now in successful conduct in their midst. They scarcely number at present, of all ages, and both sexes, more than threescore.

them. This is the miserable Situat'n of this Colony at pres't, and with't Aid from G. B., by the Infatuation and Neglect of the Assemblies on this Cont't, must rem'n a Prey in the Enemy's Depredations. The Revenue within y's Dom'n, 2s. on every Hhd. of Tob'o exported, abat'g an Allowance of 10 P C't to Masters of Vessells, for pay'g it in Bills of Exch.; 2dly, Fifteen Pence P Ton on all Ships and Vessells trad'd here, comonly called Port Duties; 3dly, Six Pence P Head on every Passenger imported; 4ly, Fines and Forfeitures for Breaches of the Penal Laws, Contempts of Courts of Justice, Breaches of the Peace, or Convict'n of Felons or Tresspasses; 5ly, Rights for tak'g up Lands, which is 5s for every 50 Acres. The three first Branches of the Revenue are appropriated by the Act of Assembly for rais'g the same, as are also the Forfeitures for Breaches of the penal Laws, for and towards the Support of Gov't, and its Contingent Cha's, and for maintaining Forts and Fortifications. The casual Fines and Forfeitures in the fourth Branch, were first appropriated to the Support of Gov't by Warr't from King Chas. the 2nd, and have continued so ever since. The last Branch of Rights for Land; was established by Order of the Gov'r and Council, in the Year 1699, to supply the defect of Importat'n Rights, on which only, People were then entitled to take up Lands, and since y't Time, it has made a considerable Addit'n to the Revenue. All these Revenue's together, amo't, Comunibus Annis, to ab't £6,500. The establish'd Exp's of Gov't, includ'g Gov'r and Council, and other Officer's Salarys, amo'ts to Yearly, as by particular Acc't below, to £4,345. The extra Exp's, Incidents, &c., are not easily to be computed, because they rise and fall as the Exigences of Gov't require, and at pres't are very high, by (reason of) Messengers, Expresses, Repairs of Gov'r's Ho., and other Incidents, as also, Alarms of Invas's from Ind's, or other great Exp's in Pres'ts to Ind's, repairing Fortificat's, and many other Affairs, that makes me incapable to fix any annual Sum on these different Dutys and Services, w'ch now amo'ts to a considerable Sum. The Establishm't now p'd out of the stand'g Revenue, are as follows:

The Gov'r's Salary P Ann	£2,000
Gent. of the Council, P Warr't	1,200
Judges and Officers of O. and Ter. Courts	200
Auditor Gen'l of Plantat's, P Warr't [6]	100
Solicitor of Virg'a Affairs [7]	200
King's Atto'y Gen'l	70
Clerk of the Council	100
Four Adjut's, each £100 [8]	400
Armourer	12
Gunners of Forts	47
An Allow'ce for Ministers to Preach Before the Gen'l Court	10

A further allowance for each Sermon Preached before the Gen-

---

[6] Then, John Blair.

[7] The agent at London, then, James Abercromby.

[8] Two of these were George Washington and George Muse, of Caroline county, at that time, field officers of the same regiment.

eral Assembly. The Rec'r Gen'l⁹ holds his Place by Pat't from H. M'Y, and is allowed 5 PCt. on all the Money he receives. The Deputy Auditor acts by Com'o. from the Auditor Gen'l of the Plantat's, and has in lieu of Salary 5 P Ct. on all the Money he audits. The Bishop of London's Comissary has an annual Salary out of H. M'y's Quit Rents, of £100 P Ann. The King's Atto'y Gen'l, has also an additional Salary from the same fund of £70 P Ann. These are the only establish'd Cha's on the stand'g Revenue. The foregoing is a true state of Dom'n of Virg'a in the different Branches of its Constitut'n.¹⁰

R. D.

No. 2

DINWIDDIE TO COL. (JOHN) BUCHANAN.

Williamsburg Augst 14th 1755.

Sirs:

Your Letter of the 8th I recd & am heartily sorry for the Death of Col.o Patton. It is a real surprise to me that the few Indians who have been in Augusta should have gone (to) so great length in robbing & murdering yr People, when I consider yr Numbers, which if they had acted with Spirit & Resolution I think they could have destroy'd them all, & protected yr Women & Children, but I fancy there has been a general Panick over the whole County; I am sorry the men you sent after the murderers did not come up with them—There is a Company of fifty men from Lunenb? (Lunenburg?) to come into yr County; yr own Company of Rangers of 50 men; another Company of 10 (40?) to be raised by Ct Smith; which Capt. Lewis's Company, I think will be sufficient for the Protection of your Frontiers, with't calling out the militia, which is not to be done till great extremity.

I am sorry to hear from you that the militia is not to be depended on or will they obey orders; which makes it obvious yt they have not been properly disciplin'd, or kept under proper command, which on refusal, you should punish them according to Law. I think some good Dogs wou'd soon find out the skulk (ing) Places of the Indians, so that the Rangers may come up with them, which I recommend to be put in Practice.

You have had more Amunition & Arms than all the other Frontier Counties together, & so it is that I cannot supply you with any more. Last week I sent Col. Lewis 200£ for the use of the Rangers. The Remains of Lieut. Wright's People, I order them to join the Company imediately, their Pay has been monthly paid & lies in Colo Wood's Hands at Winchester, where their Capt no doubt will send for it & pay his Men.

I have Letr from Col.o Lewis from Johnson's Rivr where he is doing his Duty agreeable to my orders to Col.o Patton, so I cannot charge him with Contempt or Disobedience. I have done all in my Power for the service of yr County, but if yr People will dastardly give up their Families & Interest to a barbarous Enemy without endeavoring to resist them, they connot expect to be protected, without their own Assistance against these Banditti.

---

⁹ Then, Richard Corbin.
¹⁰ Dinwiddie Papers, vol. i, pp. 380-390.

I know not whether you or Col⁰ Lewis is the senior officer in yʳ County. The Date of yʳ Commissions will show that, & he that is senior must take the Charge of the Militia for some Time, for I Shall not at present appoint any Lieutenant. Col⁰ Patton had my orders to appoint Majʳ Smith to Command the first Company of Rangers, but I find he did not do it; however he is now appointed Captⁿ of the second Company.

I cannot help the Families deserting their Habitations, if they will run away from themselves, leave their Interests, those that remain to defend the County may hereafter be thought worthy of enjoying their Plantations. I am

Sirs

Your most hole servt

ROBT. DINWIDDIE

P. S. The Lieutenancy of Counties (?) do not succeed in the Corps, but as the Govʳ pleases he apoints. (?) [11]

No. 3

A COUNCIL OF WAR, HELD AT FORT CUMBERLAND,
July 10th 1756 [12]

Colonel George Washington—President.

Lieutenant-Colonel Adam Stephen   Captain Christopher Gist
Captain Thomas Cocke   Captain George Mercer
Captain Henry Woodward   Captain William Bronaugh
Captain Robert McKenzie   Captain David Bell
Captain Henry Harrison

The President having informed the Council that the General Assembly had resolved upon building a chain of Forts for the protection of the Frontiers——To begin at Henry Enoch's, on Great Capecapon, and extend in the most convenient line to Mayo-river——the building of which forts was not to exceed two thousand pounds——and as the fixing upon the places judiciously was a matter of great importance to the Country——He desired *their* advice thereupon: and put the following Questions——

First Whether it was advisable to begin the said chain of forts at Henry Enochs's on great Capecapon:

The Council was unanimous in opinion that it was *not*——Because, as the Province of Maryland had abandoned their Settlements on Potowmack to a great distance, it left a fertile and populous district, from that down to Maidstone, at Watkins's Ferry, exposed to incursions of the Enemy; and to which there lead several warrior paths to Raystown and Susquehannah, much frequented by the Indians.

Secondly——Which was the most convenient and central place to build on, for the *protection* of that District?

The Council was of opinion that at, or near to Bendicks plantation above the mouth of Sleepy Creek was the most convenient

---

[11] Draper, MSS., Preston Papers, 1QQ86.
[12] Hamilton, vol. i, pp. 301-304 (omitted by both Ford and Sparks).

and centrical place to build a fort on for the defense of the Inhabitants on Sleepy-Creek and Back-Creek the lower parts of Opecon and Shanandoah river.

Thirdly Where ought the second Fort to be built?

The Council having considered the situation of the country and the Body of Inhabitants to be defended, are of opinion, that at or near to Henry Enochs's plantation on great Capecahon, is the most advisable place to build the second fort on.

It defends the inhabitants on the waters of Capecapon——is contiguous to the Settlements on the heads of the Waters of sleepy and back-creeks.——and maintains the communication with the Forts on Patterson's Creek, &c.

Fourthly;——Are the Forts on Patterson's Creek to be esteemed in the Line intended by the Assembly?——

The Forts on Patterson's Creek already built, and protected with several necessary houses——and the Country having more hard Service in view, than the small number of their forces can perform ——and considering likewise that to abandon those Forts, and give up so much to the Enemy would increase their insolence,——and give them a disadvantageous opinion of our strength,——The Council are of opinion that these forts are to be maintained, and reckoned in the chain intended by the Assembly.

Fifthly:——Is it then necessary to have a fort between that at Enochs and Ashby's?

To open a communication between the forts at Enochs' and Ashby's, it is necessary to clear a road leading to the South Branch above Suttons plantation, passing near to Ross's mill; from the *best* and nearest way to the fort commanded be Captain John Ashby: and as the distance will not be above twenty-two miles, it is not necessary to build between.——But the Council are of opinion a Block-house may be found necessary to secure the passage of the River.——

Sixthly——Are the Forts built by Captain Waggener upon the South Branch to be deemed in the chain intended by the Assembly?

The Forts built by Captain Waggener have had the desired effect——The inhabitants of that fertile district, keep possession of their Farms; and seem resolved to pursue their Business under cover of them.——They are therefore to be looked upon in the chain intended by the Assembly.——The Council are of opinion that it will be found necessary to maintain a Blockhouse at Pearsalls, to secure that difficult pass, and keep the communication open.

Seventhly: Which is the next important & convenient place for building on, above the upper fort, built by Captain Waggener? Upon the main branch about twenty miles higher up, where there is a considerable body of inhabitants.

The men in that Garrison may secure that Settlement, and protect those on the heads of the waters of the South Branch, and those upon Shanandoah River.

Eighthly: The President asking whether the Council in general were acquainted with the particular situation of the frontiers to the southward of the waters of the South branch?

The Council declared they were not.——And thought it advisable that the completing the chain should be referred to Captain Hogg with directions to build at or about two or thirty miles distance, as the situation of the Country requires,—or Ground will permit——And to have particular regard to the body of inhabitants to be defended and the passes most frequented by the Enemy—— and that Captain Hogg begin to build observing the above considerations,——to the southward of Fort Dinwiddie, extending the line towards Mayo river, as directed by the Assembly.

Lastly.——The Question being put——How many men were absolutely necessary for the defense of Fort Cumberland against an attack with small arms?

Notwithstanding the whole number of men raised could be employed to advantage at Fort Cumberland——yet to carry on the intended work, it was necessary to draw off as many as could be possibly spared——

The Council are of opinion that one hundred and seventy privates is the smallest number that can be left for the defense of the Garrison against small arms: and that nothing more could be expected from that number than to act on the defensive,—and do the Duty of the Garrison—with liquor and to suttle.

The President then asked whether Mr Alexander Woodrow was qualified for that office; and how he had behaved since his appointment to suttle? To which the council answered unanimously, that they thought him a very proper person and well qualified; as he has hitherto behaved with the greatest exactness and conformity to the rules and orders of the Garrison—and with much modesty and gentility.

No. 4

GOVERNOR DINWIDDIE TO COL. GEORGE WASHINGTON

Aug'st 19th, 1756.

Sir:

Your L're of the 4th I rec'd and note its Contents. I observe you have been much engag'd in setling the proper Places for the Chain of Forts propos'd to be built, and I doubt not the Places you have pitched upon are the most proper, as you know the Situation of the Country, you are the best Judge thereof. With Concern I see the Rolls of Y'r Companies, and I am sorry they are so difficient in No's; the Officers by no Means complied with their Promises and Engagem'ts when they rec'd their Commissions, and the Draught from the Militia (is) much short of my Expectation; and indeed the laying of the fine of ten Pounds on those that w'd not march out entirely defeated the Law, and was much against my Opinion, but I was glad of any law that had a prospect of augmenting the Forces, but even w'th that Inconvenience the Affairs has been poorly conducted in the different Counties. The dastardly Spirits of our lower People and the want of proper Rule in the Officers of the different Counties has been of very bad Consequence to our Affairs. I approve of Y'r Disposal of the two vacant Companies to Y'r Self and Colo. Stephens. I shall be glad (if) the Draughts made after the return of the Militia be as you desire; those from Prince William, Fairfax and Culpeper to march directly to Winchester, and please write to the Command'g Officer accordingly, as I am so much hurried that I have not time; you may write in my Name. I am sorry for the Behaviour of the Militia that were w'th Lieut. Rutherford; the Officers are difficient in keeping them under strict Commany. Till our Expedition is concerted to the Ohio Capt. Stewart's Troop must do Duty on foot, and there Pay must be reduced during that Time, and You may assure them as soon as the Troop is again form'd their Pay will be accordingly augmented as at first. The building of Forts is a necessary work, but the protecting the frontiers is more essential, therefore I w'd recommend as much as you possibly can to have Y'r Men at Call on any approaching Danger, tho' I fear it will be impracticable when divided at such a Distance, unless you appoint a proper Place for a general Rendewouse on proper Alarms given, w'ch you are the only Judge of from y'r Knowledge of the Country. If you can enlist Servants agreeable to the Act of Parliament, the Mast'r of such Sirvants shall be paid for the time they have to serve in proportion to the first Purchase, but I think you sh'd be carefull not to enlist any Convicts, who, probably, may be fractious and bad Examples to the others, and I wish they may have the desired Effect, for I cannot think of any method to raise men till the Assembly meets, and that at present is very uncertain. I am glad you have thought of Lieut. McNeel, who, I believe, is a very deserving Man. As to Fort Cumb'l'd, it's a King's Fort and a Magazine for Stores, it's not in my Power to order it be deserted, and if we did, it w'd encourage the Enemy to be more audacious when L'd Loudon comes here, w'ch, I expect, will be about the 20th of Nov'r; he has full Power to do what he thinks proper, and a Representation to him will be regular. At present it must be properly supported w'th Men, and I think from the Plan of Y'r Forts one of them is not above —— Miles distant from Fort Cumberland. I observe you mention Y'r Men want many Necessaries. I don't touch the publick Money. I shewed Y'r L're to the Speaker, and I suppose he will answer it. I told him that I think the Men sh'd be paid the full 8d. Day with't any Deduction, w'ch is agreed to, and that the new Cloathing on Arrival be given them by way of Encouragement, and I hope this Stepp will raise their Spirits and engage them to the Discharge of their Dutys w'th Alacrity. If you had sent word w't they mostly wanted they might be purchas'd here. I suppose the Cloathing will be here before Christmas. If I hear of any Opp'ty I shall send you 2 Drums, but I suppose you may have the old ones mended, and the Associators had 2, w'ch were left at Winchester or Fredericksburg, w'ch you sh'd call for. I now write to Colo. Fairfax to pay you the Bala. in his H'ds of £600. he had of me. I know nothing of Capt. Gist's Acco'ts; probably they may be w'th the Comittee. I shall be glad to do him any good Offices in my Power. The Acco't Capt. McNeel writes you about the rangers in Augusta I believe is truth, and shall take Care when they come to be paid, having several Informations to the same Purpose. I believe you will not be Summoned on Napp's Affair if Witnesses sufficient with't you can be procur'd, as I shall be glad you were here about the 20th Nov'r, when I expect the Earl of Loudon. I desire you will order Lieut. Hall down here till the 14th of Octo'r, to be evidence ag'st Mr. Hedgeman, who has treated my Character in a Villainous Manner and w'th great Injustice, and I am determin'd to make an Example of him. A great Body of Quakers waited on me in regard to their Friends w'th you, pray'g they may not be whiped; use them w'th Lenity, but as they are at their own Expence, I w'd have them remain as long as the other Draughts. I have had no proper Application in regard to the Militia that have enlisted, and if they do, I shall give little Attention to it, as from what you mention, they enlisted without any Compullsion, and took the Money with't objections or offering to return the same in 24 Hours. The Incorporating the Rangers in the Regiment will be very agreeable, if done w'th their Consent, and hope by Arguments you may prevail on them, for the Fund apropriated for paying them as rangers is exhausted; they will now receive 8d. a Day and a Suit of Cloaths, as soon as they arrive, with't paying for them. The Nottoway Indians are not return'd. I think they sh'd be p'd, to encourage the Tuscaroras to our Assistance. Mr. Timberlake, if he declines to serve as a Volunteer, must wait the Course of Preferment with the other young Gent'n. I wrote fully to L'd Loudon about an Expedition to the Ohio, but his Attention to the Affairs in the No-ward is so great that I cannot expect anything of that kind to be done this Year, but when he comes here I shall have the Opp'ty of speaking fully on that and several other Matters. I cannot tell how to prevent the Pennsylvania butchers' driving off our Cattle, unless you threaten them in a Military Manner. It's a Grievance that sh'd be amended, and therefore what present Steps you take in preventing it I will Support you therein, and no doubt Provisions must be purchased for the Regim't and the Forts. I shall speak to the Treasurer on that Subject, and a Commissary must be appointed. I shall, therefore, press the giving of Money to purchase Provisions of all kinds. I did hear of one Cheroke that was with the other Indians that took Vass's fort, and I understand there are Numbers of each different Tribe, and they assume the name of Allegany Indians. I have not heard from Maj'r Lewis since he left this (place). I sent a Messenger to the Cherokees about 5 Weeks ago, and I expect his return very soon, and I hope he will bring Nothing but what may be agreable. Pray cannot You procure a trusty Indian or two to the Twightees to endeavour to keep them in our Interest and to let them know the No. of War'rs the great King the other side of the Water has sent for our mutual Protec'n? Such a Message I conceive will be of great Service. I have order'd three forts in Hallifax and one in Bedford to be built by the Militia and Garrison'd by them some time. Colo. Stewart, of Augusta, propos'd and sent the Sketch for 14 Forts, to be Garrison'd by 700 Men, but I took no Notice of it, waiting for Capt. Hogg's Report of what he thinks may be necessary, and to be managed with Frugality, for the People in Augusta appear to me so selfish that private Views and Interest prevails with them with't due consid't'n of the publick Ser'ce w'ch makes me much on my Guard with them. I have sent up a new Commission of the Peace for Frederick County and have invited Lord Fairfax to aply to the Court for curtailing the No. of Tipling Houses, w'ch are of great Prejudice to our Men, and I hope this will have the desir'd Effect. I doubt not You sent the Drum about the Town forbiding them to trust Y'r Men or entertaining 'em in improper Hours; if guilty that you will take them on the Guard —this may probably terrify them. I doubt not you are strongly solicited for Men; on every Alarm y'r own Prudence must direct you in sending Parties out. I am weekly solicited from Augusta and the other frontier Counties to the So'ward, and I am obliged to write many L'res to the Comand'g Officers to assist the poor

11

frontier Settlem'ts. I am convinc'd from the few of Men you have that it's difficult to give Attention to all Complaints and Solicitations. The Militia that Lord Fairfax has order'd to range about Conegochege may be continued as long as you may think they are absolutely necessary. I think I have fully answer'd Y'r L're, and in what I may be difficient Y'r own Prudence must supply. Warr against France was proclaim'd here the 7th, and I order'd Mr. Walthoe to enclose you a Copy to be procliam'd at the head of Y'r Companys, and be sent to fort Cumberland; in Case of Miscarriages I send you inclos'd a printed Copy. Pray God it may be attended w'th Success in all our Operations at home and abroad. Have you order'd the Gunns at Rock Creeke to be brought to Winchester? Your Acc'ts, I think, are passed the Comittee, and I have given my Warrant for £5,000, I wish you health and Success in all Y'r Opperations, and I remain,

S'r, y'r mo. h'ble Serv't.

P. S.—When the Draughts are discharged in Dec'r y'r Number of private Men will be very few. In Course there must be a reduction of Officers, as each Company sh'd not be less than 50, but I shall speak to you on this Head when you come here.[13]

No. 5

AT A COUNCIL OF WAR HELD AT FORT CUMBERLAND
April 16th 1757 [14]

The council of war held in consequence of the non-arrival of the Maryland forces.

Present

Colo George Washington, President

Lt. Colo. Adams Stephen

Capt. Tho. Waggener	Capt Willm Bronaugh
Capt. Joshua Lewis	Capt Chas Lewis
Capt David Bell	Capt Henry Harrison

Capt. Lt John McNeill

The Colonel laid before the Council a Letter which he had just received from His Honor, Governor Dinwiddie, (dated at Williamsburgh the 7th instant:) referring him to another letter, by Express, of the 5th which had not yet come to hand——for Orders and Directions concerning the marching two hundred men to Fredericksburg by the 20th instant,——for the purpose of embarking them for Carolina——Also for the disposition of other Troops for the benefit of the frontier inhabitants: As also, concerning the sending out parties of Soldiers with the Indians. And desired their advice on the most expedient and proper measures to be used in the present situation of affairs——The Governors letter of the 7th without that of the 5th inst being altogether inexplicable.——

The Council after duly considering the Governors letter, and

---

[13] Dinwiddie Papers, vol. ii, pp. 479-483.
[14] Hamilton, vol. ii, pp. 64-65 (omitted by both Ford and Sparks).

weighing the consequences of evacuating Fort Cumberland, before the expected relief shou'd arrive: and thereby exposing the frontier inhabitants to inconceivable danger,——were unanimously of opinion

First, that Fort Cumberland shou'd not be evacuated by the Virginia troops 'till they were relieved by those from Maryland, and the Stores cou'd be removed; unless more explicit orders shou'd arrive from the Governor, requiring it.

Secondly——That the Detachment ordered to march with the Catawba Indians, to gain intelligence and annoy the enemy, ought not to be countermanded, because it might create Jealousies and uneasiness among the Indians, who earnestly desired to be accompanied by Soldiers.

Thirdly——That, as the French and Indians have already this season committed acts of hostility upon the Inhabitants; of the French; which had, together with the small force that was posted among them, discouraged the Settlers from planting, and determined a pretty large part of them to move off entirely——It is thought absolutely necessary to post troops upon the said Branch, in order to preserve that valuable settlement——to induce the people to plant a sufficiency of Corn; and to prevent by that means the vale of Winchester from becoming the Frontier.

Fourthly——That in order to this it is advisable to evacuate the Forts on Pattersons Creek (which serve no other purpose than to secure the communication between the forts Loudoun and Cumberland).

Fifthly——We humbly conceive, that the measures here proposed by this Council, are, under our present circumstances, absolutely requisite for the good of the Service, and are in no wise contradictory to anything contained in the Governors Letter of the 7th whose Intentions for want of the letter of the 5th instant, are not to be understood.

No. 6

The Loudoun Papers contain the following memorandum [15] drawn up by Governor Dinwiddie in 1757:

A LIST OF THE COUNTIES & THEIR LIEUTENANTS SUPPOSED MOST PROPER TO BE CALL'D ON IN CASE OF ANY NECESSITY

Counties				County Lieutts
Hampshire	.	.	.	Co Thos Bryant Martin
Frederick	.	.	.	Lord Fairfax

[15] The document is endorsed by Loudoun in this way: "List of Lt. of Countys in Virginia with Lt Go Dinwiddies letter of May 18th 1757" (Loudoun Papers, List of Counties, 1757, May). The county lieutenant in colonial Virginia governed the county and upon him rested the responsibility of a faithful execution of the laws. He was usually a large landed proprietor and was commonly styled "Colonel." He could call out the militia when their presence was demanded and was accountable to the governor and council for his conduct. The officers of the militia were subject to his orders and he had authority to organize courts martial.

Counties				County Lieutts
Augusta	.	.	.	Majr Andrew Lewis
Albemarle ·	.	.	.	Co Pat. Jefferson
Louisa	.	.	.	Colo Robt Lewis
Orange	.	.	.	Co Geo. Taylor
Culpeper	.	.	.	Co Slaughter
Spotsylvania	.	.	.	Co Jno Spotswood
Fairfax	.	.	.	Co Wm Fairfax
Prince Wm	.	.	.	Co Henry Lee

No. 7

DINWIDDIE TO THE EARL OF LOUDOUN, DECEMBER 24, 1757 [16]

The enclos'd Letter from the Council I am desired to forward You, which I do by this Express; it chiefly relates to the 50,000 £ granted by Parliament to the two Carolinas & this Dominion & we believe left to Your Lordship in Proportion to the Service each of these Colonies have done for his Majesty & the Common Cause & no Doubt Your Lordship will distribute that Sum in an equal Manner agreeable to the Merits of each different Colony.

As I am going to leave this Government, I think it my indispensable Duty to acquaint Your Lordship that this Colony has rais'd upwards of 200,000£ for His Majesty's Service, & kept in pay a Regiment ever since the Commencement of Hostilities, which I am convinc'd is attended with above three Times the Charge & Expense of the other two Colonies mention'd in the Grant by Parliament——The Money & Credit sent me has chiefly been expended in Genl Braddock's Time, & in Presents &c to the Ins & the Accts have been transmitted to the Treasury.

The Legislature readily obey'd Your Orders in sending Forces to So Carolina, with Powder & Lead from the Magazine; in short, my Lord, I must do the Country the Justice to say, that they have been more ready than any of the others in supporting the Common Cause, & I doubt not You will readily agree that they are entitled to a greater Share of that generous Donation, & they are very glad that it's left to Your Lordship's Distribution.

The Country is now much in Debt & wants many Necessaries for the Public Service from Home, & they have great Dependence on this Money to qualify them to make the proper & necessary Supplies; & I hope you will excuse my writing so fully on this Affair, which is done as my Duty & the Regard I have for this Dominion.

No. 8

"BLAIR" REPORT ON THE STATE OF THE COLONIES [17]

July 20, 1756.

To the King's Most Excellent Majesty
May it please Your Majesty——

As it appeared to be of the greatest Importance, at a time

---

[16] Loudoun Papers, Dinwiddie file, L. S., 1757 (omitted from published Dinwiddie Papers).

[17] Manuscript report on the state of colonial defense prepared

when Your Majesty judged it necessary to take vigorous Measures for Asserting and Maintaining Your just Rights and Possessions in America, and for protecting Your Subjects there against the Encroachments of a foreign Power, that Your Majesty should be truly and exactly informed of the State of Defense of Your several Colonies and Plantations, We thought it Our Duty in September last to direct the respective Governors thereof to prepare and transmit to Us, with all possible dispatch, an Account of the actual Quantity and State of the Cannon, Small Arms, Ammunition, and other Ordnance Stores belonging to their respective Governments, either in the publick Magazines or in the Possession of the Militia, or other private Persons, as also the true State of all Places either already fortified or which they should judge necessary to be fortified, together with their Opinions respectively in what manner Your Majesty may further contribute to the Defense and Security of such Colony, and having lately received Returns from Your Majesty's Governors of New Hampshire, Rhode Island, New York, New Jersey, Pennsylvania, Virginia, Georgia, Jamaica, the Leeward Islands, and the Virgin Islands, We humbly beg leave, without delay, to lay the same before Your Majesty and shall think it Our Duty humbly to represent to Your Majesty the State of Defense of the rest of Your Majesty's Colonies and Plantations, so soon as We shall have received the like Returns from the respective Governors of them.

VIRGINIA

With regard to the present State of Defense of Your Majesty's Colony of Virginia, Robert Dinwiddie Esqre., Your Majesty's Lieut. Governor, in his Letter of the 23 of February last, informs Us, that there are three Forts in the said Colony Vizt.

1. Fort George, at the Mouth of James River, on which were formerly mounted ten Cannon of 24 pounds, 6 of 12 pounds, and four of 9 pounds, But the Fort having been built on a bad Foundation the Sea has undermined it, and dismounted all the Guns, which having been Sent thither in the Reigns of Queen Elizabeth & King Charles, are become honycomb'd, and unfit for Service, and now lie buried in the Sand.

2d. A Fort at the Town of York on York River mounting eleven Guns of 18 and nine pounds, and ten small Guns of a pound, and half, of which the large Guns are all honycomb'd and unfit for Service.

---

by Dinwiddie and the other English governors; forwarded by them to the Lords of Trade in London, and by them transmitted to King George II. These highly important reports are contemporaneous evidence as to the actual and deplorable conditions throughout all the colonies. And as an aid in unraveling the story of Virginia's part in the French and Indian War they are almost indispensable. It is clear from these candid reports that England and her colonies beat the French in spite—not because—of the condition of colonial defense in the thirteen provinces. This considerable manuscript, hitherto unpublished, is a part of the papers of John Blair, prominent colonial Virginian and for a time president of the council, and is temporarily referred to in the Huntington Library as the "Blair" Report.

3d. A Fort at Gloucester on the same River, mounting 15 Guns of 18, 12 and 6 pounds, but, like the others, unfit for Service.

These Forts Mr. Dinwiddie represents as very properly situated, and of great importance to the Security of the Colony, as they command the Entrance of two of it's most considerable Rivers, But he Observes that the Batteries, altho' considerable Sums have been expended on them, Yet for want of a Skillfull Engineer to direct the Construction of them, and particularly of the Foundations, are in a very ruinous Condition.

As to the Ordnance and Military Stores in this colony, Mr. Dinwiddie informs Us, that there are 250 whole Barrels and 180 half Barrels of Gunpowder, 17 Bags of Shott of about 30 Cwt., 8 small Bags of Flints, 28 Halberts and 12 Drums; But there are no small Arms left, he having sent 400 to the late General Braddock, 1300 to New York and New Jersey, and distributed 800 to the Soldiers now in the Pay of the Colony.

With regard to the Militia of Virginia, Mr. Dinwiddie acquaints Us, that having, upon his Arrival in his Government, found the Militia in very bad Order, he appointed four Adjutants, to four different Districts of the Country to teach the Officers their Duty, and to train the private Men to the use of Arms; That by the Returns of these Adjutants the Militia amounts to about 36,000, but not above half that Number are arm'd, and the Arms of those who have any are of different Bores, which is inconvenient in time of Action. He adds that he has endeavour'd to prevail on the Assembly to vote a general Tax to purchase an uniform and compleat Set of Arms for the Militia, to be lodged in Magazines in each County, and delivered out as Occasion may require, but as Yet he has not been able to succeed.

For the Number of Inhabitants, Whites & Blacks within Your Majesty's said Colony, Mr. Dinwiddie has transmitted to Us a List of Tithables White and Black, Copy whereof We humbly beg leave to annex, from which it appears, That white Tithables are only the Males of 18 years of Age and upwards, & Women and Males and Females under 18 Years, which are not tithable, are computed at four times the Number of Tithables so that the Number of White Tithables being 43,329, the Total Number of White Inhabitants, upon such Computation, will be 173,316.

It appears also from the said List, that Negroes, both Male and Female are tithable, at the Age of sixteen Years and upwards, and those under that Age being computed to be of equal Number, the whole Number of Blacks within the said Colony is 120,156.

With regard to what further may be necessary for the Defense and Security of Virginia, and in what manner Your Majesty may contribute thereto, Mr. Dinwiddie is of Opinion:

1. That it is absolutely necessary that the 3 Forts should be rebuilt under the Direction of a Skillfull Engineer to be sent from hence, and furnished with a sufficient Number of good and serviceable Cannon, vizt:

> For Fort George,
>   25 Cannon, 24 pounders.
> For York Battery,
>   15 Cannon, 18 pounders.
> For Gloucester Fort,
>   12 Cannon, 18 pounders.

But he observes, that the Colony has no money to apply to these Services, the fund of two shillings phh'd on Tobacco, which is appropriated to the Ordinary and extraordinary Contingences of Government, having been so entirely exhausted by the late Exigencies, that there hardly remains in the hands of Your Majesty's Receiver General a Sufficiency to answer the Ordinary and unavoidable Expenses of Government, and he despairs of Obtaining any money for these purposes, however necessary from the Assembly.

2.   That a Fort should be built at Cape Henry, which commands the Entrance from the Sea to Virginia and to Maryland, for which 20 cannon of 24 pounds will be requisite with a proportionate Quantity of Ordnance Stores.

3.   That as the Frontiers of Your Majesty's said Colony to the Westward are 300 Miles from North to South, and the distance from any part of the Colony that is tolerably peopled to the most Westerly Settlements being about 200 miles, the Militia cannot give timely assistance to the back Inhabitants against any sudden Incursions of the Enemy, He is of Opinion that Forts should be built along the Ridge of the Allegany Mountains, at those Passes, thro' which the Country is accessible and garrison'd with a competent Number of Soldiers.

As the Ordnance necessary for these Forts, Mr. Dinwiddie observes, that of the 30 Cannon of four pounds, which Your Majesty was graciously pleased lately to send thither, ten have been mounted at Fort Cumberland, a Fort erected within the Limits of Maryland; ten more were by Order of the Late General Braddock sent to Rock Creek at the head of Potowmack River, to be ready to be mounted on the Fort on the Ohio, if he had taken it, and the remaining ten, which now are at Hampton at the Mouth of the James River, may be applied as part of the Ordnance, which will be requisite for the Forts he proposes to be erected on the said Ridge of Mountains.

A LIST OF TITHABLES IN THE DOMINION OF VIRGINIA.
APPENDIX NO. 9.

Counties	Whites	Blacks	Counties	Whites	Blacks
Accomac	1,506	1,135	King Geo	720	1,068
Amelia	1,251	1,652	Lancaster	486	1,124
Albemarle	1,344	1,747	Louisa	655	1,452
Augusta	2,273	40	Luneburg	1,209	983
Brunswick	1,299	976	Middlesex	371	1,056
Bedford	357	143	Norfolk	1,132	1,408
Chas. City	537	1,058	Nansemond	989	1,264
Caroline	1,208	2,674	No'ampton	609	902
Chesterfield	841	1,198	New Kent	465	1,209
Culpeper	1,221	1,217	No'umberland	980	1,434
Cumberland	704	1,394	Orange	627	1,016
Dinwiddie	784	1,175	Princess Ann	840	880
Eliz'h City	316	812	Prince Geo	650	1,138
Essex	889	1,711	Prince W'm	1,384	1,414
Fairfax	1,312	921	Prince Edw'd	416	410
Frederick	2,173	340	Richmond	761	1,235
Gloster	1,137	3,284	Surry	587	1,006
Goochland	569	933	Stafford	889	1,126
Henrico	529	898	Spotsylvania	665	1,468

Counties	Whites	Blacks	Counties	Whites	Blacks
Hanover	1,169	2,621	So'hampton	973	1,036
Hampshire	558	12	Sussex	778	1,388
Halifax	629	141	Westmoreland	944	1,588
James City	394	1,254	Warwick	181	665
Isle of Wight	810	966	York	562	1,567
King & Queen	944	2,103			
King W'm	702	1,834		43,329	60,078

OBSERVATIONS ON THE TITHABLES.

The White Tithables are only the Males from 18 Years and upw'ds. Women and those under the Age of 18, both Males and Females, are not tithed, and from best Informt'n they may be computed at four times the Number of Tithables that is 43,329 multiplied by four makes 173,316, the whole No. of Whites in y's. Dom'n. The Negroes or Blacks are Tithable from the Years of 16 and upwards, both Males and Females, and under y't Age they are not subject to be tith'd, therefore I think the No. of Black Tithables may be doubl'd: y't is to say, 60,078 with the young Negroes at the above Calculat'n will amo. to 120,156, the full No. of Slaves in y's Colony added to the Whites makes 293,472 the compleat No. of Inhabitants.[18]

"To the King's Most Excellent Majesty
May it Please Your Majesty——

Since our Representation to Your Majesty dated the 11th of May last, wherein We humbly laid before Your Majesty an Account of Several of Your Majesty's Colonies and Plantations in America, and of what further the respective Govrs of such Colonies judge necessary for their more effectual Defense and Security, We have received the like Accounts from the Governor and Company of the Colony of Connecticut, from the Lieut. Governor of the Province of Maryland, & from Your Majesty's Governors of the Province of North Carolina and of the Bermuda Islands, which we beg leave in like Manner humbly to lay before Your Majesty.

The Governor and Company of Connecticut in their Letter dated the 30 of March last, informs Us with respect to the actual State of Defense of that Colony, that at the Harbour of New London there is a Battery of Nine Guns, 3 of which are unfit for Service, and that there are three more useless pieces of Cannon at the entrance of the Port.

The report proceeds to explain the provision in the laws of the colony whereby each town was obliged to keep 50 pounds of powder, 200 pounds of bullets, and 300 flints for each sixty enlisted soldiers; each and all others exempted from duty must keep in their homes and show to the proper officers on the first Monday in May annually the following: "One Gun and Sword or Cutlass. one pound of Powder, four Pounds of bullets, and one dozen of Flints."

MARYLAND

Then follows an account of the "State" of Maryland. The province was reported to have nineteen carriage guns, all iron

---

[18] Loudoun Papers, Blair Report (Lords of Trade to the King), July 20, 1756.

and in good condition, four of them being 6-pounders and fifteen 4-pounders not mounted. The stores of ammunition contained sixteen hundred-weight of 6-pound shot, and smaller quantities of miscellaneous supplies.

The white inhabitants of Maryland are reported by Governor Sharpe as 107,963; the blacks at 46,225. Of the whites, the governor "computes about 26,000 able to bear arms, but all Civil Officers and Persons of particular Trades or Callings being exempted by Law, convicted Servants incapacitated, and Roman Catholicks excluded or excused by Custom. The Militia does not exceed 16,500, or one-third of whom are entirely destitute of Arms, and many of the Musquets, that are the Property of the rest, are very bad and scarcely fit for use; and for want of a proper Militia Law, (which the Assembly have in vain been frequently solicited to make), the People are undisciplined as well as badly arm'd, and cannot be compell'd to serve in Defense of the Country.

"There are no Works in this Province that deserve the Name of Fortifications. Behind & amongst the most Western Settlements are some small Stockadoes or palisaded Forts, which may serve for the Protection of the Women and Children, in Case of Alarm, while the Men unite and endeavor to prevent any small Parties of Indians making incursions and destroying their Stock and Habitations.

"Besides these there is one large Fort (but in Mr Sharpe's Opinion not much more capable of Defense) on Potowmack River about 46 Miles beyond the said Settlements, called Fort Cumberland. This Fort is made with Stockadoes and commanded almost on every side by circumjacent Hills. It is at present garrisoned by 400 Men from Maryland and Virginia, and Ten of the Carriage Guns, which Your Majesty was graciously pleased to order to Virginia two Years since, are mounted on it.

"Mr Sharpe further informs us, that about sixteen Miles on this side of Fort Cumberland there is an Eminence situated at the Conflux of the two Streams call'd the North & South Branches of Potowmack, and almost as far up as that River is navigable for the smaller Craft, which might be easily fortified, and at a small expense. He is of Opinion" that it ought to be fortified, properly to defend the contiguous parts of the two neighboring colonies and be given a proper garrison.

NORTH CAROLINA

"Arthur Dobbs Esquire, Your Majesty's Governor of North Carolina, in his Letter of the 15th March, has transmitted to Us a List of the Militia and taxable Persons, (which are White Males of 16 Years and upwards, and Negroes of both Sexes of 12 Years and upwards in the several Counties of that Province, and an Account of the quantity of Powder and Lead in the Hands of the Collectors of the several Ports, Copies whereof We humbly beg leave to annex."

Governor Dobbs reported the number of the militia to be that of the preceding year inasmuch, he explained, as he could not obtain the present year's returns in time for the desired report. He reported further "that not half of the Militia are arm'd, (and) as no Supply of Arms can be got, altho' they would willingly purchase them . . . that there is some Gunpowder received by the Powder Duty, of which he has not yet obtained an account from the Collectors, but the quantity is not yet sufficient to supply the Militia, far less to allow any to the Forts."

He reported, moreover, "that the Fort at Cape Fear is not tenable," though it is now being repaired, "there is neither Garrison, Ammunition, Arms, nor Cannon, except a few Ship Guns which are unfit for Service . . . ; that two Batterys are now erecting . . . the one at Cavebanks near Ocacock Bar, and the other at Newtopsail inlet; the Assembly having granted the Sum of £4,000 North Carolina Currency for the first of these Services and £1,500 for the latter."

"That the Assembly have also granted £1,000 for erecting a Stockadoed Fort on the Western Frontier at a place which is fix'd on near the Catawba's River. . . ."

"Besides the Forts and Batteries above mention'd Mr Dobbs is of Opinion that it is absolutely necessary that a Fort should be erected at Cape Lookout as proposed in his Letter of the 19th of May 1755, which We laid before their Excellencies the Lords Justices in our humble Representation of the 29th of July last. He observes that it is the safest Harbor between the Cape of Florida and Boston in New England; that Ships may lie there landlocked from all Winds; may (take on) Wood, Water, and clear . . . as was practiced by the French and Spaniards in the last war. . . ." The governor asks that this place be fortified, and garrisoned with 300 men in time of war and 100 in time of peace.

BERMUDA (omitted)

NEW HAMPSHIRE

Benning Wentworth Esqr, Your Majesty's Governor of New Hampshire has transmitted to us two Accounts (copies of which are hereunto annexed) . . . (omitted) Wentworth reported that while "the Batteries of William and Mary are well placed" . . . "that three of their Batteries, which were erected during the last war, have thro' Neglect gone to decay, and will be of little or no Service, till they are repaired, which he has no hopes of getting done by any Grant from the Assembly; specially as the necessary Repairs of Fort William and Mary will require a Sum of money much beyond the Abilities of the People under their present Taxes. That Warlike Stores of every kind are extremely Scarce in His Government, that hardly a Regiment of the Militia in the Province is fully provided with a Pound of Powder to each Man, which is the Quantity with which the Law requires each Soldier to be furnished, and that it would be difficult to fit out 100 Men, without breaking in on Your Majesty's Stores." Wentworth proceeds to advise the Home Government that as the Province has "ever" been exposed to Indian incursions, the "Militia both Horse and Foot are esteemed more usefull for Home Service than those of the Southern Colonies, and that they are most provided with Arms but in general of the meanest Sort."

RHODE ISLAND

"The Governor and Company of Your Majesty's Colony of Rhode Island in their letter dated the 24th of December 1755 gave us the following accounts of its actual State of Defense." This portion of the report proceeds with a description of the location of the colony, calling attention to the fact that it is water-bounded and open to attacks by sea. Then it continues: " On a small Island (harbor of Newport) lying before it, at the distance of about half a Mile, stands the only Fort or Fortification that now is or ever has been in the Colony. . . ." There are now, he reports, 5,265 enlisted soldiers in the colony, comprising four regiments of fifty-three companies, and two troops of horse. These troops are trained twice yearly. At the semi-annual muster, each soldier is required to bring musket, sword, and a pound of powder with ball and other stores in proportion, and for neglect is fined 40s for each day. Moreover, every able-bodied man, though not an enlisted soldier, is obliged to keep arms and ammunition in his house. All told, there were reported to be 2,997 men able to bear arms, exclusive of the militia. But, " as about 1/8th part of them are People call'ed Quakers, who on Account of Religious Principles refuse all military service, the Number to be depended on for the defense of their Country must be considered as so much less." The governor recommends that the fort at Newport be made stronger, that more arms be sent, and as the colony did " in the last year expend on the said Fort and in the Expedition to Crown Point more than £20,000 Sterling " he begs that the colony be reimbursed in an equal amount to repay them for their expenditure.

NEW YORK

"Sir Charles Hardy, Your Majesty's Governor of New York, in his Letter dated 16th January last, has transmitted to us Returns of all the Cannon in that Province and of all the warlike Stores in Fort George (copies of which are hereunto annexed)." The cannon and supplies are so scarce that it was " with difficulty " that the governor " could furnish Fort Edward upon Lake George with the few which are now there from the Fort at Albany, and that these left in it are not safe in firing. . . . He informs us, that many Cannon of a smaller size will be wanting for Out-Forts and Blockhouses; and he has hopes for Forts in the Indian Castles, as those Nations seem inclined to have such built for their Security. He adds that there are no small arms in the Publick Magazines except six chests that belong to the four independent Companies. That the City of New York has a stand of 1,000 Muskets, which they provided last year, and the Arms which are in the Possession of private People are chiefly for Indian Trade. That the Militia (of which he has not as yet been able to learn the exact Number) are by Law required to furnish themselves with a good Musket and a due proportion of Ammunition each Man; but that Some of them are so indigent, that they cannot purchase their proper arms."

NEW JERSEY

" Your Majesty's Province of New Jersey appears to be in the most naked and defenseless Condition. For Jonathan Belcher Esqr, Your Majesty's Governor, in his Letter dated the 5th of December last, acquaints us, that there, no Cannon, Small Arms, or other ordnance or military Stores belonging to the said Province, and that there is not, nor (as he inform'd) ever was in all the Province, one Fortification or Place of Defense. That he has recommended it to Your Majesty's Council to consider, What may be necessary to be done for the Defense and Security of the said Province, and in what manner Your Majesty may contribute thereto, and when he has received their Advice, he shall make a further Representation to Us thereupon." As to the number of inhabitants and militia, " Mr Belcher informs Us, That there may be above 80,000 Whites, of which about 16,000 may be able to bear Arms, and that the number of Blacks is computed to be between 15 & 1800. That from the return made the last Year by the Colonies of the several Regiments, the Number of the Militia appear'd to be about 13,000 effective Men, who are Obliged by Law of the Province to be muster'ed and trained every six months, and to appear every Man, with a good Firelock &c, fit to march against an Enemy."

PENNSYLVANIA

" We have so lately had Occasion fully to state to Your Majesty the naked and defenseless State in which the Province of Pennsylvania is and always has been, and the Source of this Evil, that it appears unnecessary to lay before Your Majesty what Mr Morris, the Lieutenant Governor of the Province, writes to us upon those general Points. But with regard to its present State he informs Us, That toward the close of the late War, some of the most considerable of the Inhabitants, who by the Consent and Approbation of the Government enter'd into an Association, purchased Arms & formed themselves into Regiments and Companies, did, by voluntary Subscription, erect a Battery upon the River Delaware near the South end of the City, upon which they planted 46 Cannon of 18 and 24 pounders, 12 of which were given by the Proprietors, and the remainder were purchased by the Members of the said Association. This Battery has since been suffer'd to go to decay, and is not yet repaired, but it is proposed soon to repair it. That a great part of the money granted by the Act for granting £60,000 to Your Majesty's Use, pass'd in November last, has already been laid out in building a Line of small Forts or Blockhouses on the long extended Frontier from Delaware to the Maryland Line near the River Potomack (which work is almost compleat) and in paying, arming and subsisting about 1,000 Men, who are form'd into Companies and station'd at those Forts, with Orders by Detachments to range and scour the Woods each way from their respective Posts to prevent the Indians from penetrating into the Settlements, which are for the most part within the Line of these Forts; But altho' these Forts are erected and garrisoned, yet as there is no Law to inforce Military Obedience, without which it is impossible to keep either officers or Soldiers to their Duty, or even to retain them in the Publick Service, when it becomes disagreeable; and as there are no hopes of obtaining such a Law from An Assembly, who have declared they think all Compulsion in matters of that sort unlawful, the Lieutenant Governor far from thinking the Province in such a Posture of Defense as its Situation and Circumstances require, is apprehensive, that the whole £60,000 will be thrown away to very little purpose for want of a proper and equitable Militia Law, which, however just and necessary it may be, he is certain can never be obtain'd from the Legislature of that Province as now constituted, and until it is obtained, the Province in his Opinion can never be effectually defended. Upon the whole therefore, Mr Morris observes, that Pennsylvania, tho' a considerable Colony with more than 40,000 fighting Men in it, is in no Condition to defend itself, but must fall an easy Prey to almost any Invader, unless the British Parliament shall be pleased to interpose, and, by proper Laws, establish Order and Discipline among the People, and thereby enable them to defend the Country they possess.

(Signed)

Whitehall   Dunk Halifax [19]
July 20th, 1756   James Oswald
                                       J. Talbot
                                       W. G. Hamilton."

---

[19] George Montagu Dunk, second Earl of Halifax, became president of the Board of Trade, 1748.

MANUSCRIPT SOURCES.

I.—Draper Manuscripts. State Historical Society of Wisconsin. Madison.

    Preston Papers (QQ). (6 volumes). A calendar of the series was published by the State Historical Society of Wisconsin in 1915, see pages, 1-147. For the purposes of this study, see volume 1, 1757; volume 2, 1758-1773; volume 6, 1757-1766, a military receipt book for Preston's and Buchanan's companies.

    Virginia MSS (ZZ). (16 vols.). A calendar of this series was included in the above publication in 1915, see pages 147 ff. For this study, see volmes 1, 3, 4, 5, 14, 16.

    Bedinger MSS (A). 1 volume.

    Draper's Life of Boone (B). (5 vols.). Volumes 1, 2, 5.

    Boone MSS (C). (33 vols.). Volumes 1, 2, 3, 4, 5, 25, 32.

    Border Forays (D). (5 vols.). Volumes 1, 2.

    Brady and Wetzel MSS (E). (16 vols.). Volume 1.

    Brant MSS (F). (22 vols.). Volumes 1, 2, 17, 18, 19.

    Brant Miscellanies (G). (3 vols.). Volume 1.

    George Rogers Clark MSS (J). (65 vols.). Volumes 1, 46, 57.

    George Rogers Clark Miscellanies (K). (5 vols.). Volume 1.

    Jonathan Clark Papers (L). (2 vols.). Volume 1.

    Draper's Historical Miscellanies (Q). (8 vols.). Volumes 1, 5, 7. Volume 7 comprises clippings from English newspapers (1758-1801). The American items (found on pages 1-56) relate chiefly to military affairs during the French and Indian and Revolutionary wars. The English intelligence is quite miscellaneous in character. (List 18).

    Draper's Notes (S). (33 vols.). Volumes 10, 11, 12, 13, 14, 15, 16.

    Frontier Wars MSS (U). (23 vols.). Volumes 1, 3, 10, 11, 12, 21.

    Kenton MSS (BB). (13 vols.). Volume 1.

    Newspaper Extracts (JJ). (4 vols.). Volumes 1, 2.

    Potter Papers (PP). (1 vol.). Volume 1.

    The character and extent of the Draper Manuscripts are set forth in the Descriptive List of the Manuscript Collections of the State Historical Society of Wisconsin. Edited by R. G. Thwaites, 1906. The contents of an important portion of those utilized in this study are indicated in the Calendar of the Preston and Virginia Papers. Calendar Series, vol. 1. Edited by M. M. Quaife, 1915.

    In the description and citation of documents the following classification has been observed:

    Papers: The original documents of any person or group of persons, or those connected with any historical event.

    MSS: Materials concerning a person, including both original documents and facts collected from descendants and other sources.

    Notes: Unassorted materials concerning a person or event, collected by letters, personal interviews, etc.

    Miscellanies: Miscellaneous printed material concerning a person or event.

In the references the marginal pressmark indicates the location of the original document in the Draper Collection. The number before the letters shows in which volume of the series the document occurs, the letters designate the series, while the number following the letters indicates the page or pages of the volume occupied by the document. To illustrate, the Pressmark 1QQ92 means that the document is found in the Preston Series, volume 1, page 92. This particular reference is to the list of the company of rangers of Captain William Preston, Augusta County, Virginia, giving date of enlistment, nationality, age, size, trade, and date of discharge or desertion. A. D. 1 page. Endorsed. July 16, 1755, to January 1, 1756. A. D., autograph document; A. D. S., an autograph document signed; D. S., document signed.

II.—WASHINGTON MANUSCRIPTS. Library of Congress. (4 vols.).

III.—HUNTINGTON COLLECTION.

The Henry E. Huntington Library at San Marino, California, contains among other valuable materials the Brock Collection of Manuscripts, including the Dinwiddie Papers, brought West recently from Virginia; the Loudoun, Abercrombie, and other important papers acquired from depositories in England.

A great quantity of printed material, general, state and local, has been employed in the course of this research. The titles of the chief contributors are to be found in the footnotes.

INDEX

Abercromby, James, Virginia agent in London, 37-38, 44, 44n.

Adams, John, speech in favor of Washington, 87.

Agent of Virginia colony, 44n.

Albany Congress, 1754, 62, 63; Virginia representation at, 64.

Albemarle, Earl of (William Anne Keppel), 44.

Alexandria, Virginia, conference of governors at, 68.

Amherst, General Jeffrey, orders Forbes to proceed against Fort Duquesne, 89; orders Colonel Montgomery to relieve Fort Prince George, 94; plans campaign against Cherokees, 94.

Appalachian Mountains, 16, 17.

Armstrong, Capt. Thomas, 100.

Ashby, Capt. John, 112, 158.

Ashby, Nimrod, 122-123.

Assembly, story of Dinwiddie's relations with, 24-28; colonial governors versus assemblies, 29-30; Dinwiddie's first address to, 32; sets up buffer colonies, 33-34; second session of, 34; discord in second session, 36; effect of "pistole fee" dispute on, 38; third session of, 38, 53, 54; attempts to supervise expenditures for frontier, 41; dissolution of, discussed, 41; fourth session convened, 42, 57; prorogation of, 42; vote of £500 to Dinwiddie, 46; Dinwiddie not unpopular with, 46; fifth session of, 58; sixth session of, 59; fails to send commissioners to Albany Congress, 64; supposition as to attitude, 71; votes £40,000 for defense, 73; votes to maintain regiment, 1760, 94; provides for chain of forts, 100.

Atkin, Edmund, appointed to management of Indian affairs, 107.

Augusta Court House, council of war held at, 1756, 100; now Staunton, Virginia, 100.

Augusta County, topography of, 21; Mississippi River in, 33; county-lieutenant of, 73; frontier of Virginia, 74; ravaged by Indians, 74, 85-86; boundary line of, 138-139; people in, condemned by Dinwiddie, 161.

Austin, Wallace, 112.

Bacon, Lt. John, 111.

Baker, Lt. James, 116.

Belcher, Jonathan, governor of New Jersey, 66.

Bell, Capt. David, 125, 157, 162.

Bingaman, Samuel, 125.

Blagg, Capt. John, 142.

Blair, John, comprehensive report on the state of the colonies, 1756, 164-173.

Block-houses, 99-100.

Bouquet, Colonel Henry, repels attack against Fort Pitt, 1763, and marches against the Indians, 96, 97.

Braddock, General Edward, 14, 21, 25, 60, 65, 67, announcement of coming, 59; story of famous expedition, 68-71; criticism of leadership, 71n.; carried off field, 133.

Breckenridge, Captain Robert, 100, 124.

Brockenborough, Lieutenant Austin, 116.

Bronaugh, Captain William, 116, 125, 157, 162.

Brown, Major John, 100.

Buchanan, Colonel John, president of council of war, 100; visits Ft. Brackinridge, 113; member of council of war, 118; house at Luney's Ferry, 146; important letter of Dinwiddie to, 156-157.

Buckner, Lt. Mordecai, 108, 116, 125.

12   177